**The Pulpit and the
Christian Calendar** *1*

Books in the Stephen F. Olford Biblical Preaching Library

The Pulpit and the Christian Calendar 1

Preaching on Significant Days

Stephen F. Olford

BAKER BOOK HOUSE
Grand Rapids, Michigan 49516

ISBN: 0-8010-6716-2

Second printing, March 1992

Printed in the United States of America

These resources were adapted from material published by the Institute for
Biblical Preaching, Box 757800, Memphis, TN 38175-7800.

The New King James Version is used as the basis for this Bible study. Occasion-
ally the King James Version (KJV) is used.

The author is grateful to the many copyright owners for the use of their material.

Contents

Introduction

I recall that it was a Thanksgiving Day service. At the time, it was our custom to celebrate this seasonal event with a 10:30 A.M. service at Calvary Baptist Church in New York City. It happened to be a *very* popular event in the life of our church. Not only did our members attend, but we attracted many friends and visitors as well.

Contrary to my usual practice, I had trusted a guest speaker for this particular year. As he was from overseas I carefully explained to him what Thanksgiving meant in the United States and suggested that he should take an appropriate subject to fit the occasion. As it turned out, however, my preacher-friend chose otherwise! He delivered a sound, but strange, sermon on "The Wrath of God!" What followed can only be described as disaster! Some people left as he was preaching, while others sat in silent puzzlement and disappointment. In short, it was not a *thanksgiving service*, and a great opportunity was lost. I could only pray that God, in his sovereignty, would overrule for his own purpose and bless even one soul.

Perhaps the greatest blessing that year was the important lesson that I learned! Failure to exploit seasonal occasions with sanctified sensitivity is not only foolish, it is fatal!

Now as my readers will know, our Christian calendar year is trinitarian; hence, we have New Year with its suggestions of "beginnings," and God the Father as Creator and Originator of all things. Then we have the Lenten period, Good Friday, and Easter Sunday with its reminders of God the Son as Redeemer and risen Lord. This is followed by Whitsun (or Pentecost) when we think of God the Holy Spirit in all the wonder of his power and blessing. Finally, we come to Christmas with its emphasis on the incarnation and the glory of our Immanuel. In between these periods we have, in our American culture, Sundays that honor mothers, fathers, labor, veterans, and so on. While our ministry cannot be bound by or restricted to these seasonal occasions, we must use what I have called "sanctified sensitivity" and adapt accordingly.

This particular volume is devoted to the pulpit and the Christian calendar. Needless to say, we cannot cover every event in the calendar, but there are expository sermon outlines that can be starting points for your preparation and proclamation. We cannot study our Lord or the apostles without discerning their powers of adaptation in given situations of life. This is the essence of good preaching!

So I exhort you to "preach the word! . . . [and] do the work of an evangelist," but also to "preach the word . . . in season *and* out of season . . ." (2 Tim. 4:2, 5). God bless you and make you a blessing.

Stephen F. Olford

Part 1

New Year's Sunday

1

God's New Thing
Isaiah 43:18–21

"Behold, I will do a new thing; now it shall spring forth"
(43:19, KJV).

Introduction

Some time ago one of our leading newspapers reported a suicide on the first day of a new year. The victim was an eighteen-year-old girl. Before she took her life she left a note which read, "I made an agreement with God that *unless* life was worth living I would quit living." Here was a young lady who decided that she wanted life worth living, but on her own terms. But alas, she found "doing her own thing" utterly dissatisfying and ultimately destroying.

By way of contrast, life is worth living for those who delight *in the Lord*—for he promises to satisfy the desire of every heart. He transforms despondency into expectancy.

He says, "Behold, I will do a new thing; now it shall spring forth." What a text for a new year! In its sweep it offers:

I. The Promise of God's New Thing

"Remember ye not the former things, neither consider the things of old. Behold, I will do a new thing; now it shall spring forth" (43:18–19). There is a divine seed of hope in these words, for God is telling us that he is about to do a new thing. Indeed, he states his intention in terms of a promise.

A. God Promises to Transcend the Things That Are Past

"Remember ye not the former things, neither consider the things of old" (43:18). That statement may not grip us until we look into the context and find that the "former things" refer to the mighty works of God, in the liberation, preservation, and occupation of his people. He was able to say, "I am the LORD your God, the Holy One of Israel, your Savior; I gave Egypt for your ransom" (43:3). In that one phrase, "I gave Egypt for your ransom," we have the whole story.

Illustration

Illustrate with the story of the exodus from Egypt and the entrance into Canaan.

B. God Promises to Transform the Things That Are Present

"Thus saith the LORD, your redeemer, the Holy One of Israel; For your sake I have sent to Babylon, and have brought down all their nobles, and the Chaldeans, whose cry is in the ships. I am the LORD, your Holy One, the creator of Israel, your King. . . . which bringeth forth the chariot and horse, the army and the power; they shall lie down together, they shall not rise: they are extinct, they are quenched as tow [or "as a wick"]" (43:14–17, KJV).

These verses go beyond the deliverance from Egypt to the deliverance from Babylon. How sad it is to recognize that a nation that had proved God in liberation, preservation, and occupation should now find themselves captives once again in Babylon. But this is exactly what happened. Because of their backsliding and rebellion God had to send them in judgment down into Babylon. But in answer to the prayers of a faithful remnant a great deliverance was effected.

Amplification

Amplify from the context to show that through God's miraculous working there can be a life of *spontaneity*—"I will do a new thing . . . it shall spring (or sprout) forth" (43:19); a life of *creativity*—"I will . . . make a way in the wilderness" (43:19); and a life of *productivity*—"I [will] give waters in the wilderness, and rivers in the desert" (43:20).

II. The Purpose of God's New Thing

"I will do a new thing. . . . I [will] . . . give drink to my people, my chosen. This people have I formed for myself; they shall shew forth my praise" (43:19–21, KJV). In this prophetic language we have devotional truth. When God redeems us it is for a purpose, and if we have eyes to see, that purpose becomes the supreme goal of our lives.

A. God's Purpose Is to Satisfy His Own People

"I give waters in the wilderness . . . to give drink to my people" (43:20). God's greatest delight is to satisfy his people. He says: "Blessed are they which do hunger and thirst after righteousness: for they shall be filled"

(Matt. 5:6, KJV). God wants to do a new thing in our lives—spiritually, mentally, emotionally, volitionally, physically, and vocationally.

Illustration

Illustrate how God satisfies the longing heart, by citing the experience of David (see Ps. 27:3–7, 25, 37).

B. God's Purpose Is to Magnify His Own Person

"This people have I formed for myself; they shall shew forth my praise" (43:21, KJV). From Genesis to Revelation this truth shines forth with increasing brilliance. Peter sums it up perfectly when he says that we are "a chosen generation, a royal priesthood, an holy nation, a peculiar people; that [we] should shew forth the praises of him who hath called [us] out of darkness into his marvellous light" (1 Peter 2:9, KJV). Jesus said the same thing when he said, "Let your light so shine before men, that they may see your good works, and glorify your Father which is in heaven" (Matt. 5:16, KJV). This is why God says, twice over, in this very chapter, "Ye are my witnesses" (43:10, 12). Let us never forget that "man's chief end is to glorify God and to enjoy him forever."

III. The Prospect of God's New Thing

"But thou hast not called upon me, O Jacob; but thou hast been weary of me, O Israel. Thou hast not brought me the small cattle of thy burnt offerings. . . . Thou hast bought me no sweet cane with money, neither hast thou filled me with the fat of thy sacrifices." And then he goes on to say in language that is just music to the soul: "I, even I, am he that blotteth out thy transgressions for mine own sake, and will not remember thy sins. Put me in remembrance; let us plead together: declare thou, that thou mayest be justified" (43:22–26). If we are to enter into the promise and purpose of God's new thing in our lives then we must recognize certain facts. Indeed, there is no prospect of realizing God's new thing without perceiving two things of utmost importance:

A. The Failure of Man to Cope

"But thou hast not called upon me, O Jacob; but thou hast been weary of me, O Israel. Thou hast not brought me the small cattle of thy burnt offerings; neither hast thou honoured me with thy sacrifices. I have not caused thee to serve with an offering, nor wearied thee with incense. Thou hast bought me no sweet cane with money, neither hast thou filled me with the fat of thy sacrifices; but thou hast made me to serve with thy sins . . ." (43:22–24).

These verses make sad reading, but they are a true reflection of the failure of man to cope or come to terms with God. In the final analysis, we have to recognize that God can only expect utter failure from us.

Amplification

Amplify the aspects of this failure by showing how God's ancient people failed in *intercessions*—they had not called upon the God of Israel; *dedications*—they had mocked him with their burnt offerings and sacrifices; and *ministrations*—God had to say to them, "Thou hast made me to serve with thy sins, thou hast wearied me with thine iniquities" (43:24).

B. The Nature of God to Care

"I, even I, am he that blotteth out thy transgressions for mine own sake, and will not remember thy sins. Put me in remembrance: let us plead together: declare thou, that thou mayest be justified" (43:25–26). In simple terms, this teaches us that God is waiting to forgive our sins, to purge our iniquities, and to blot out our transgressions. More than that, he offers in their place a new faith. He says, "Put me in remembrance" (43:26). In the Hebrew, this literally means "to bring back to mind the promises on which we can agree."

Illustration

Illustrate from the life of Paul. Recall the times of crisis in his life when even his friends forsook him, but—"notwithstanding the Lord stood with [him]" (2 Tim. 4:17; see also Acts 23:11; 27:23). God always kept his promise.

Conclusion

Let us believe God for his new thing in our lives, then go forth to prove his adequacy in the coming days. And let us remember that with God the best is yet to be.

2

The New Start
Philippians 3:12–16

"Forgetting those things which are behind, and reaching forth unto those things which are before, I press toward the mark for the prize of the high calling of God in Christ Jesus" (3:13–14, KJV).

Introduction

The month of January is named after the Roman god Janus, who was usually depicted as a man with two faces. One face looked back into the year that had passed and that face bore traces of sorrow, dismay, and perplexity; the other, forward-looking, personified hope and confidence.

At this time of the year one cannot help looking back; many of us traditionally take stock at the opening of a new year. Has the past year been one of fear and anxiety? Then you need to read the words of the apostle Paul in Philippians 3:13–14: "Brethren, I count not myself to have apprehended: but this one thing I do, forgetting those things which are behind, and reaching forth unto those things which are before, I press toward the mark for the prize of the high calling of God in Christ Jesus." In simple terms, Paul tells us that:

I. We Should Forget the Things Which Are Behind Us

"This one thing I do, forgetting those things which are behind" (3:13). One of the great barriers to making a new start is the horror of the past. Failures, as well as successes, constantly harass us until we are afraid to attempt anything new. If we would forget the things that are behind us:

A. Past Sins Must Be Forgiven

"Forgetting those things which are behind" (3:13). There can be no forgetting without forgiveness, for "God requireth that which is past" (Eccles. 3:15). Paul was doubtless conscious of the many failures and sins in his life. The way he had blasphemed the name of Jesus and persecuted the church of God must have haunted him day and night. But the time came when he owned up to his sins and, having confessed them, entered into the experience of forgiveness and cleansing.

In a similar way, if we would know a fresh start in our lives we must experience the forgiveness of our past sins. Thank God, the Bible says, "If we confess our sins, he is faithful and just to forgive us our sins, and to cleanse us from all unrighteousness" (1 John 1:9).

Illustration

"Forget the things that are behind: forget injuries, slight, unkind words; be too big to be hurt; be too great to be unkind; be too busy to quarrel; too wise to engage in unseemly gossip; too strong to permit little annoyances to turn you from life's big road; too clean to stain your character with any kind of impurity."[1]

For example, "those inventive people, the Italians, have a custom. As midnight on New Year's Eve approaches, the

streets are clear. There is no traffic; there are no pedes-
trians; even the policemen take cover. Then, at the stroke
of 12, the windows of the houses fly open. To the sound of
laughter, music, and fireworks, each member of the family
pitches out old crockery, detested ornaments, hated furni-
ture and a whole catalogue of personal possessions which
remind them of something in the past year they are determined to wipe out of their minds."[2]

B. Past Successes Must Be Forsaken

"Forgetting those things which are behind" (3:13).
Employing the metaphorical language of the race course,
Paul speaks of leaving behind the previous stages of the
race. He implies that he must not waste time surveying
his progress; only one thing is important, that is, running to win.

One of the most subtle devices of the enemy for slow-
ing us down in our Christian lives is that of engaging
our minds and hearts with the memory of past successes. If we are going to live lives of present holiness
and victory, we must of necessity concentrate more on
today than on yesterday.

Illustration

When Sir Winston Churchill visited the United States
during World War II he was heard to say that "if the present
quarrels with the past there can be no future." The point he
was making was that we have to accept the past as un-
alterable and move on from there. To stay and quarrel with
it, or be preoccupied with it, is to ruin the future.

Paul had a most eventful and illustrious past, but he
realized that to be preoccupied with it was to divert his
focus from the present.

So let us make sure that our past sins are forgiven
and that our past successes are forsaken. Only then shall
we step out into a new life in Christ.

II. We Should Foresee the Things
Which Are Before Us

"Reaching forth unto those things which are before, I press toward the mark for the prize of the high calling of God in Christ Jesus" (3:13–14). The apostle Paul has at least two important objectives in mind. In essence, we can describe them as the eventualities of life and the responsibilities of life. Let us consider each of these.

A. The Eventualities of Life

"Reaching forth unto those things which are before" (3:13). Most people are afraid of the future. Uncertainty and insecurity about the days that lie ahead fill the heart with fear and foreboding. But for the Christian, there need be no fear. In the language of the old hymn, he can say with Edward H. Bickersteth:

> Peace, perfect peace, our future all unknown?
> Jesus we know, and he is on the throne.

There is nothing that can ever happen which is not already foreknown and included within the permissive will of God. There is a sense that through trust in the living God we can foresee the things which are before us. The eventualities of life need neither terrify nor disturb us.

B. The Responsibilities of Life

"I press toward the mark for the prize of the high calling of God in Christ Jesus" (3:14). The picture is still that of the runner whose eyes are on the finish line. No one can ever make a success of life without having a goal before him. Someone has said that "if you aim at nothing, you are sure to hit it."

The apostle Paul points out that the goal of every Christian should be "the prize of the high calling of God in Christ Jesus." Without doubt, the prize is the reward at the judgment seat of Christ. What greater achievement in life can any believer foresee than that of being crowned that day! The great apostle could say as he neared the end of his race: "I have fought a good fight, I have finished my course, I have kept the faith: Henceforth there is laid up for me a crown of righteousness, which the Lord, the righteous judge, shall give me at that day: and not to me only, but unto all them also that love his appearing" (2 Tim. 4:7–8).

Amplification

Amplify to show that the responsibilities of every Christian involve *righteous living in the present day*. This is "the prize of the high calling of God in Christ Jesus" (3:14). This "high calling" is also termed "a holy calling" (2 Tim. 1:9). Such a quality of life demands separation and consecration worked out in everyday experience. This means following the Lord Jesus, whatever the cost. This righteous living is crowned with *rewarded living in the future day*. There is a "prize" to win in that future day. How we live here on earth will determine our status and authority in a coming day, when Jesus shall reign undisputed over the universe. The Bible tells us that "if we suffer, we shall also reign with him: if we deny him, he also will deny us" (2 Tim. 2:12). It is a solemn fact to contemplate that throughout eternity we will carry with us the evidences of having been faithful or unfaithful here upon earth. It is important to foresee what is before us, if we would live righteously and rewardingly.

III. We Should Fulfill the Things Which Are Beyond Us

"Not as though I had already attained, either were already perfect: but I follow after, if that I may apprehend that for which also I am apprehended of Christ Jesus" (3:12). Commenting on this passage, Dr. M. R. DeHaan says: "Self-satisfaction is the death of progress. Dissatisfaction with past accomplishments is the mother of invention. Because man was dissatisfied with carrying and lifting loads upon his shoulders, he invented vehicles to ride in. Pity the man who is content with his own progress and feels he has [arrived]. This is all the more true in the Christian life. Nothing here is as deadly as self-satisfaction. The most boring people I ever meet are the ones who take up my time telling me what they have *done*, when they ought to be *doing more*."[3]

Illustration

"An officer rode up to the general, saluted, and said proudly, 'Sir, we have just taken two gun emplacements from the enemy.' He waited for the compliment of the general, expecting him to say, 'Very good, now you can take a rest.' But instead, the general curtly ordered, 'Go back and take two more.'"[4]

In the life of faith we move from strength to strength, we abound more and more, we proceed from glory to glory.

Perfection, for the apostle Paul, was nothing less than being conformed to the image of the likeness of Christ. This is why he declared his greatest ambition in those unforgettable words: "That I may know him, and the power of his resurrection, and the fellowship of his sufferings, being made conformable unto his death" (3:10). To know Christ and to be made like him we must experience:

A. His Resurrection Power

"That I may know him, and the power of his resurrection" (3:10). The resurrection power of Jesus Christ is that divine dynamic which raised him from the dead, conquering all the powers of sin and Satan. For us, to know this resurrection power is to be able to live in constant victory, which Paul affirms when he says, "I can do all things through Christ which strengtheneth me" (Phil. 4:13).

Illustration

"A godly Church of England vicar was troubled with a violent and apparently ungovernable temper. Many a time he had prayed about it with tears, and he had struggled much to conquer it, but had been beaten and was almost in despair. One day he had prayed and confessed his sin and believed he had obtained help to keep down the violent temper, and so he had left his study to go about his duties. Alas! not long afterward he reentered his study beaten and almost brokenhearted, and in his sorrow he fell asleep and dreamed he was in his study and, looking out, saw coming toward him a glorious man who evidently intended to be his guest. He became at once conscious that his study was in much disorder and unfit to receive such a guest, who, he knew, was the Lord Jesus Christ. He swept and watered and dusted the room, but the more he worked the worse it became. The stranger knocked. 'Oh, what shall I do,' he said to himself. 'I cannot let him into a room in such disorder as this,' and he kept on sweeping, watering, and dusting till the stranger knocked again, and again he said, 'Oh, I cannot open while the room is so unfit to receive him.' But all his efforts were in vain, and when the stranger knocked again, overpowered with shame and confusion, he opened the door, saying, 'Master, I can do no more; come in if thou wilt into such a room.' The Master came in, and, most strange, when he came in the dust was laid, the disorder disappeared, and all was bright and clean and joyful. The Master's presence alone had done all that his utmost efforts had failed to accomplish. He awoke, and it was a dream, but in the dream God had spoken to him, and he now saw where his mistake had been, and wherein lay his strength for an overcoming life."[5]

B. His Redemptive Passion

"That I may know him . . . and the fellowship of his sufferings, being made conformable unto his death" (3:10). This is more than suffering for Christ, it is suffering with Christ. Indeed, it is the highest form of suffering, for it is sharing with the risen Lord a redemptive passion for a lost world. None of us can know this redemptive passion without being concerned with the needs of our fellow men, the chaos of the present world, and the desperate need of getting out the gospel with its message of forgiving love.

Illustration

> If you would plant for a year:
> Plant grain;
> Yours will be an ear
> Of grain.
>
> If you would plant for a decade:
> Plant trees;
> Yours shall be olives and shade
> And ease.
>
> To plant for eternity:
> Plant men;
> Eternal harvest shall be
> Yours then.
>
> Ralph Keesar

If we would know a redemptive passion we need to pray with utmost sincerity the words of Amy Wilson Carmichael:

> O for a passionate passion for souls;
> O for a pity that yearns;
> O for a love that loves unto death;
> O for a heart that burns![6]

Conclusion

All these and more are involved in starting a new life, from the Christian's point of view. So I invite you to forget what is behind, to foresee what is before, and to fulfill what is beyond you, enabled by the power and passion of a living Christ. Whatever your life has been in the past, rejoice in the knowledge that you can start afresh!

Part 2

Lent

3

The Centrality of the Cross

1 Peter 2:13–25

"Who Himself bore our sins in His own body on the tree, that we, having died to sins, might live for righteousness— by whose stripes you were healed" (2:24).

Introduction

The cross of our Lord Jesus Christ is the outworking of God's redemptive purpose in time and in eternity. For this very reason the cross is central in God's Word as well as being central to God's world. In the Bible we find the mes- *①* sage of the cross of Christ central in the Law, the Psalms, the Prophets, the Gospels, the Acts, the Epistles, and the Book of Revelation. To remove this recurring truth is to render the Bible meaningless. But the cross is also central *②* to God's world. It was planted on a hill called Calvary in a land called Palestine. The cross is central in history, for *③* the death of Christ divides human history and is the converging point of two eternities.

But, supremely, the cross of Christ is central to human experience, having an important relevance to the relationships of government and people, masters and servants, husbands and wives. A careful study of these verses makes it obvious that without submission to the Christ of the cross there can be no hope of peace, harmony, or good will. The reason for this will become clear in the passage before us. According to Peter:

I. The Cross Is God's Standard for Men

"For to this you were called, because Christ also suffered for us, leaving us an example, that you should follow His steps" (2:21). The word "example" means "something written underneath," "traced," or "copied over." The verb translated "you should follow" is a compound one, suggesting a close following of the example already given. Peter recalls the example of the Lord Jesus and sees in the life and death of the Savior God's standard for all men. Observe that the standard of the suffering Savior was one of:

A. Absolute Sinlessness

Christ ". . . committed no sin, nor was guile found in His mouth" (2:22). Although Peter is here quoting from the Old Testament (see Isaiah 53), he is choosing His language carefully. No one followed the Lord Jesus more closely or knew him more intimately than Peter. Therefore, as he reviews that life and death, he says, he ". . . committed no sin, nor was guile found in His mouth" (2:22). Jesus never failed in deed nor in word; he was guilty of neither error nor deceit. This means, of course, that Jesus did not deserve to suffer or die; but as a Lamb without blemish and without spot he suffered and died for men and their salvation. Only a sinless Savior could atone for sinful men.

Illustration

At the close of an evangelistic service a gentleman approached Dr. D. M. Stearns with a criticism, "I don't like your way of preaching. I do not care for all this talk about Christ dying for the lost. Instead of preaching the death of Christ on the cross it's better to be up-to-date. Preach Jesus, the teacher and example." "Would you then be willing to follow him if I preach Christ as the great example?" asked Dr. Stearns. "I would," said the gentleman. "I would follow in his steps." "Then," Dr. Stearns said, "let us take the first step: 'Who did not sin,' as we read in 1 Peter 2:22. Can you take this step?" The critic seemed confused. "No," he said, "I do sin, I must admit." "Well, then," said Dr. Stearns, "your first need of Christ is not as an example, but as a Savior."[1]

B. Absolute Submissiveness

". . . who, when he was reviled, did not revile in return; when he suffered, he did not threaten, but committed himself to him who judges righteously" (2:23). The emphasis in this verse is on the surprising silence of Jesus as well as his submission to treatment that he never deserved. When unjustly reproached he did not answer back; when unfairly treated he did not condemn his oppressors, or invoke judgment upon them. In the language of the prophet Isaiah, "He was oppressed and he was afflicted, yet he opened not his mouth . . ." (Isa. 53:7). Someone has written:

> Why is He silent when a word,
> Would slay His accusers all?
> Why does He meekly bear their taunts,
> When angels wait His call?
> "He was made sin," my sin He bore
> Upon the accursed tree,
> And sin hath no defense to make
> His silence was for me.[2]

We cannot contemplate the Savior's behavior in suffering and death without being amazed at his sub-
missiveness. This is the example God has set before
us in the relationships of government with people,
masters with servants, husbands with wives. But the
objector says, "This can't be done! If this is what God
expects we are hopelessly lost!" Of course, the answer
is that we *are* hopelessly lost! This is why God says,
". . . all have sinned and fall short of the glory of God"
(Rom. 3:23). Only as we measure ourselves against
God's standard do we realize our desperate need for
God's salvation.

II. The Cross Is God's Salvation for Men

". . . who himself bore our sins in his own body on the
tree, that we, having died to sins, might live for righteousness—by whose stripes you were healed" (2:24). The
only reason why God sent his Son to die upon the cross
is because there was no other way to remove the guilt of
sin and to save the souls of men. If there were any other
way of salvation, God—in his infinite wisdom and power—
could have certainly devised it. This is why the cross is
most crucial and central in God's purpose of redemption.
Observe carefully that God's salvation means:

A. Deliverance from the Penalty of Sin

". . . who himself bore our sins in his own body on
the tree . . ." (2:24). Here is the clearest statement concerning the purpose of the death of Christ. Whatever
theories may surround the doctrine of the atonement
one thing is inescapable: Christ died for our sins when
he hung upon that tree. The whole description in this
verse is spectacular and dramatic. Peter is giving his
testimony as an eyewitness of an event in history, point-
ing out that the one who died to put away sin was none

other than Christ himself. He emphasizes "who Himself bore our sins in His *own body* on the tree . . ." (2:24). Jesus did nothing less than take our penalty *"right up onto the tree,"* as the original has it. No one else could have done this.

Illustration

One afternoon in 1975 Daniel Waswa, a citizen of Kenya, East Africa struggled up a hill and was crucified by his wife at his own direction. As he hung on the cross, he told the gathered crowd: "I am dying for the sins of all Kenyans." After nailing her husband to the cross, the woman collapsed and died, apparently from shock. Waswa's neighbors knew this was no spur-of-the-moment act. He had talked about it for a year and had told them he had been called by God for this purpose. They begged him to let them take him down. He refused all requests. Finally, he was taken down still alive, but he soon died of the nail-wounds, which had become infected. A tragic sacrifice offered in vain, wherein two died! There is only one sacrifice by which mankind may live—Jesus himself.[3]

B. Deliverance from the Power of Sin

". . . we, having died to sins, might live for righteousness . . ." (2:24). We cannot study these words without reaching the conclusion that the purpose of Christ's passion was not only to deliver us from the penalty of sin, but also from the power of sin. We might add that as we come to appreciate the death of Christ we cannot do anything else but hate sin and love righteousness. Peter uses a word here which does not occur again in the whole of the New Testament. He tells us that we are to be dead to sin and alive unto righteousness. The word "dead" means "removed from" and was used by Greek writers to describe the departed or the dead. The idea Peter has in mind is that through the cross of Christ we have no more connection with our old sin or with a life of sinning. By the power of the

risen Lord we are now to separate ourselves from sin-
fulness and dedicate ourselves wholly to righteousness.
What a difference this would make to all our relationships of life!

C. Deliverance from the Poison of Sin

". . . by whose stripes [we] were healed" (2:24). While
Peter is quoting here from Isaiah 53:5 he also has in
mind the unmerciful scourging of the Lord Jesus. He
can still visualize those lacerations on the Savior's body,
so he declares, ". . . by *whose stripes* [we] were healed"
(2:24). Sin is not only a matter of guilt and power in our
lives, but also of poison which affects the whole of our
personalities. Sin is a sickness for which there is only
one antidote: it is the precious blood of the Lord Jesus
Christ. His life laid down in death and taken up again in
resurrection cleanses, purifies, and heals.

Have you by faith appropriated this great salvation
God has provided in his Son? Have you laid hold of his
deliverance for the penalty, power, and poison of sin?
Until you do, you are lost, for this is the only standard
that God accepts; this is the only salvation which makes
any sense in time or in eternity.

III. The Cross Is God's Satisfaction for Men

"For you were like sheep going astray, but have now
returned to the Shepherd and Overseer of your souls"
(2:25). In his inscrutable wisdom, God has made provision not only for our salvation, but for our satisfaction. It is
one thing to be saved, it is another to realize all that God
has designed for our redeemed humanity, so we need both
a Savior and a Shepherd (see v. 25). Two thoughts suggest
themselves:

A. The Shepherd Restores the Soul

". . . the Shepherd . . . of your souls" (2:25). Without doubt, Peter has Psalm 23 in mind where David says, "The LORD is my shepherd; I shall not want. He makes me to lie down in green pastures; he leads me beside the still waters. He *restores* my soul . . ." (23:1–3).

Even after our salvation there is a tendency to wander and stray. Indeed, until the day of our final redemption we will possess a perverse nature which can be overcome only by the indwelling life of Christ. Therefore, at any point that we decentralize our faith from Christ to ourselves we can fail again. This is where our Shepherd comes along to restore our souls. The thought is more than restoration from sin: it involves a restoration to a peace "which surpasses all understanding" (Phil. 4:7); a joy which is ". . . inexpressible and full of glory" (1 Peter 1:8); a hope which is "sure and steadfast" (Heb. 6:19); and a love which is ". . . as strong as death . . ." (Song of Sol. 8:6). Restoration, therefore, is fellowship with God and with fellow saints. There is nothing more satisfying in all the world than to know soul restoration. As St. Augustine exclaimed, "Our souls were made for God and we are restless until we find our rest in him."

B. The Shepherd Preserves the Soul

". . . the Shepherd and Overseer of your souls" (2:25). If restoration is the negative aspect of the Shepherd's ministry, then preservation is the positive aspect of this same ministry. Writing to the saints at Thessalonica, Paul prayed for the preservation of their total personality. ". . . the God of peace Himself sanctify you completely," he says, "and may your whole spirit, soul, and body be preserved blameless at the coming of our Lord Jesus Christ" (1 Thess. 5:23). It is a glorious thought to contemplate that under the care of the Shepherd and Overseer (or bishop) of our souls we can be preserved blameless until Jesus Christ comes again and our work on earth is done. Paul had this confidence for himself, for he could say, ". . . I know whom I have believed and am persuaded that He is able to keep what I have committed to Him until that Day" (2 Tim. 1:12; see also John 10:28).

Illustration

Full Coverage

I have an insurance policy
Written in the blood of the Lamb,
Sealed by the Cross of Jesus,
Redeemable wherever I am!

The company will never go bankrupt,
It is bonded by God's promise true;
It will keep every word of its contract,
Exactly what it says it will do.

I don't have to die to collect it,
No premiums do I have to pay;
All I do is to keep God's promise
And walk in his holy way.

No collector will ever come calling,
It was paid on Calvary's tree;
It insures me for living and dying
And for all eternity.[4]

H. H. Hover

Conclusion

We have seen what we mean by the centrality of the cross of Christ. It is God's standard for men, it is God's salvation for men, and it is God's satisfaction for men. Outside of the cross of Christ God has nothing to say to a sinful world; its message to us is one of deliverance and assurance. Come in repentance to that cross, and by an act of faith make the Christ of that cross central to every relationship of your life. Only then will you know the healing and harmonizing streams that flow from the place called Calvary.

4

The Claims of the Cross
Matthew 27:27–32

"... Him they compelled to bear His cross" (27:32).

Introduction

Once the sentence of death was pronounced, we are told that Jesus was led forth to Calvary, bearing his cross. So great was the strain and suffering of the preceding hours and so heavy was his wooden load that the Roman soldiers feared his complete collapse. We read that "... they found a man of Cyrene, Simon by name. Him they compelled to bear His cross" to Golgatha's hill (27:32). Three considerations demand our attention:

I. The Compulsion of the Cross

"... Him they compelled to bear His cross" (27:32). The word "compelled" is of ancient origin. It was used of Persian couriers who had the authority, at a regular stage in the journey, of commandeering anyone they deemed suitable to carry precious cargo or correspondence to a desired destination.

Whether or not Simon was a disciple of Jesus at this point is not revealed. What is clear, however, is that the compulsion of the cross demanded:

A. A Change of Direction

". . . as they came out, they found a man . . ." (27:32). Mark tells us that Simon was ". . . coming out of the country" (Mark 15:21). From that point onward he traveled in a different direction; this was the spiritual turning point in Simon's life. No one can bear the cross of Christ without experiencing a revolutionary change. Jesus said, ". . . if anyone desires to come after Me, let him deny himself, and take up his cross daily, and follow Me" (Luke 9:23). Simon's desires and designs that day had to be denied for Jesus Christ. Bearing the cross always means saying no to self and yes to Christ.

B. A Change of Devotion

Luke records that ". . . they laid the cross [on Simon] that he might bear it after Jesus" (Luke 23:26). How suggestive this is! Bearing the cross and following Jesus are the essence of Christian devotion. Jesus taught that unless a person was willing to bear the cross and follow him he could not be his disciple (see Luke 14:27). Discipleship denotes desire, discipline, and devotion.

As we contemplate the compulsion of the cross we need to ask ourselves whether we have faced its demand upon our lives. Has the cross changed the direction and devotion of our lives?

Illustration

A man came back from a weekend retreat experience
and when a friend asked him how it was, he said, "I died!"
The friend asked him what he meant. "You see," the man
answered, "I went to this thing not knowing what to expect.
But in the process of that long weekend, I discovered that
I had spent my whole life hiding behind a lot of masks. I
realized that I had never even let my wife see me as I really
was. I'd been playing games with her, and playing games
with my children, and playing games with others—never
letting anybody know what I really am. The worst of it was to
discover that I didn't even know myself. I was not in touch
with my own honest feelings about myself. And, as all of
this was being exposed over the weekend, I died over and
over again." It is a painful thing for a middle-aged man to
discover that he is not even in touch with his own honest
feelings about himself. "I am convinced," he said, "that I
had to go through this death experience in order to become
the new person that I hope to be now." Unless a grain of
wheat falls to earth and dies, it remains alone. But if it
dies, it bears much fruit.[1]

II. The Costliness of the Cross

". . . Him they compelled to bear *His cross*" (27:32).
Simon literally carried the cross that day. He felt its curse,
its weight, its pain, but even more important, Simon
became identified with the threefold costliness of the
crime:

A. The Shame of the Cross

It is said of the Lord Jesus that ". . . for the joy that
was set before Him [he] endured the cross, despising
the shame . . ." (Heb. 12:2). There is such a thing as the
shame of the cross. Paul calls it ". . . the offense of the
cross . . ." (Gal. 5:11). The word "shame" means "to
cover up." It is the reaction to exposure and vulnera-

bility. Never was a man in history more exposed and vulnerable than Simon on that first Good Friday.

To be identified with Jesus Christ is to be put into the open; and man does not like that! In his unregeneracy—and even carnality—he prefers the darkness. As Jesus taught: ". . . this is the condemnation, that the light has come into the world, and men loved darkness rather than light, because their deeds were evil" (John 3:19). But once a man takes up the cross, the days of secrecy are over. He goes further to endure the cross, despising the shame.

B. The Suffering of the Cross

". . . Him they compelled to bear His cross" (27:32). As the weight of that wooden load sank into Simon's shoulder, he experienced suffering. What was physically true of the Cyrenian must be spiritually true of you and me. Peter tells us that ". . . Christ also suffered for us, leaving us an example, that [we] should follow His steps" (1 Peter 2:21). Etymologically speaking, the word "suffering" means "to bear the weight." Jesus bore our sins, our sorrows, our sicknesses in a complete and atoning sense. In this respect we can never follow him. However, in the outworking of what he has done for us we can have a share. This is what Paul means when he speaks about filling up ". . . what is lacking in the afflictions of Christ, for the sake of His body, which is the church" (Col. 1:24). George MacDonald has written: "The Son of God suffered unto death, not that men might not suffer, but that their sufferings might be like his." This "fellowship of suffering" (Phil. 3:10) is sharing the Savior's redemptive concern for a world of sin, sorrow, and sickness. It is dying to our selfishness and living by his selflessness. Paul could say, "always carrying about in the body the dying of the Lord Jesus, that the life of Jesus also may be manifested in our body. For we who live are always delivered to death for Jesus' sake, that the life of Jesus also may be manifested in our mortal flesh. So then death is working in us, but life in you" (2 Cor. 4:10–12).

Illustration

The proprietor of a dry cleaning and dyeing business hung this quaint sign in his window: "We dye to live, we live to dye; the more we dye, the more we live; and the more we live, the more we dye." For the child of God, it is also true that the more he dies, the more he lives.[2]

C. The Sacrifice of the Cross

". . . Him they compelled to bear His cross" (27:32). Simon could never have carried that cross all the way to Calvary without lingering to see Jesus give himself in sacrificial death. Ever after he could say with Paul, ". . . the Son of God, who loved me and gave Himself for me" (Gal. 2:20).

So the sacrifice of the cross is giving one's body and blood in redemptive service. It is holding back nothing for the glory of God and the good of man. No demand will be too great for the believer who personally knows something of the claims of the cross upon his life. C. T. Studd, that famous cricketer and missionary of a bygone generation, made these words his motto: "If Jesus Christ be God, and died for me, then no sacrifice is too great for me to make for him."

Illustration

When James Clavert went out to cannibal Fiji with the message of the gospel, the captain of the ship on which he traveled sought to dissuade him. "You will risk your life and all those with you if you go among such savages," he said. Clavert's magnificent reply was, "We died before we came here." And yet he would have been the last to talk about a sacrifice; it was not a life of sacrifice, but of real pleasure.[3]

Have you counted the cost of bearing the cross? If you had been Simon of Cyrene would you have accepted that wooden load to bear it after Jesus?

III. The Compensations of the Cross

". . . Him they compelled to bear His cross" (27:32). We know very little of the subsequent life of Simon of Cyrene, but what is disclosed is full of instruction and inspiration. We learn, for instance, that God is no man's debtor. We cannot bear the cross in vain; there are the compensations of the cross.

Illustration

When Sir Walter Raleigh spread his beautiful new cloak over the mud so that queen Elizabeth might walk without getting her shoes dirty, he was shrewd enough to know that nothing is lost that is given to royalty. Indeed, in a very true sense, it is impossible really to deny one's self for our King. His return is so swift and so vastly in excess of what we give. But it is the heart of self-sacrifice that he wants.[4]

For Simon, this meant:

A. The Blessing of the Cross in the Home

Mark recalls that Simon of Cyrene was ". . . the father of Alexander and Rufus . . ." (Mark 15:21). This man was so transformed by the power of Christ that the blessing of the cross overflowed to his home. Mark refers to his two sons, Alexander and Rufus, as well known believers in the Christian church. "It is tempting, in view of the tradition that Mark's gospel is Petrine preaching as it took shape at Rome, to see a possible reference to the Rufus of the Roman church."[5] Paul certainly acknowledges Rufus as a man ". . . chosen in the

Lord . . ." and his mother (Simon's wife) as a mother in
the Lord to the great apostle (Rom. 16:13). What a home
this must have been! Today, the only answer to the problems of the home is cross-bearing. Only when the power
of the cross penetrates the relationships of husband and
wife, parents and children, is there authority, stability,
and security in the home.

B. The Blessing of the Cross in the Church

When Luke enumerates the leaders who taught and
ministered in the church at Antioch, he names ". . .
Simeon who was called Niger . . ." (Acts 13:1). Many
scholars maintain that this is our man. Indeed, some
suggest that he was a black man since he came from
Libya in North Africa and was surnamed Niger. If these
suppositions are correct then Simon became one of the
greatest blessings in the life of the early church. As Alan
Cole puts it: "Simon of Cyrene might be taken homilet-
ically as a picture of every disciple, bearing the Lord's
cross for him."[6]

How we need men of the cross in the church of Jesus
Christ today! Only where Calvary is a reality is sin
judged, self-crucified, and the Spirit outpoured.

C. The Blessing of the Cross in the World

". . . Him they compelled to bear His cross" (27:32).
We can never compute the blessing which Simon has
become to the world since that first Good Friday.
Throughout the centuries the story of cross-bearing, at
the moment of our Savior's greatest need, has converted
and inspired millions. In this sense, Simon has been
honored above Peter, James, John, or any other disciple
who forsook the master and fled, leaving him to carry
his cross alone.

Conclusion

Jesus still calls for cross-bearers. To heed his call is to become a blessing to your generation in the home, in the church, and in the world. We cannot adequately present a crucified Christ without a crucified life, and crucifixion, in terms of personal living, is bearing the cross, accepting its claims upon our lives. Before we shrink from this holy responsibility let us remember that Jesus took up the cross in the first place in order that we might be pardoned from our sins and quickened by his Spirit. Now he asks us to share its shame, suffering, and sacrifice in order that its redemptive power might be released through our lives to the world that we represent. No wonder Jesus said, ". . . whoever does not bear his cross and come after Me cannot be My disciple" (Luke 14:27). Once we have faced this challenge of cross-bearing we are left with one of two choices: either to be a disciple or a deserter. God give us the grace to follow Simon of Cyrene who took up the cross and bore it after Jesus.

5

The Crime of the Cross
Mark 15:1–15

"For he [Pilate] knew that the chief priests had handed Him over because of envy" (15:10).

Introduction

The sin of envy—one of the seven deadly sins mentioned in Scripture—is the outstanding crime of the cross. Envy is evil under every guise, but especially so when garbed with the vestments of pretentious piety. The fact that envy can and does penetrate the boundaries of religious life should come as a salutary warning to every heart. A threefold picture of this green-eyed monster is given us in this chapter which is sufficient to send us to the cross for deliverance. As we consider the context let us observe:

I. The Conception of the Sin of Envy

"For . . . [Pilate] knew that the chief priests had handed Him over because of envy" (15:10). According to that Greek scholar, W. E. Vine, envy is "the feeling of displeasure produced by witnessing or hearing of the advantage or prosperity of others." Almost without exception, this is the bad sense in which the word is used throughout the New Testament, but it does not reveal the motivating power behind this malicious evil. Only as we examine the events that led up to that first Good Friday and then carefully analyze our text do we see that the conception of envy is theological, both in its implication and application. In other words:

A. Envy Is the Rejection of the Deity of Jesus Christ

". . . [Pilate] knew that the chief priests had handed Him over because of envy" (15:10). Only a matter of weeks earlier the Lord Jesus had performed the greatest of all his miracles, that of raising a man to life again after he had been buried for four days. Such was the testimony of Lazarus to this remarkable miracle that the fame of Jesus spread far and wide (see John 11:47–53). Everybody knew that a miracle like this could only be performed by God, but these Jews did not want to acknowledge this fact (see John 3:2). They said to Pilate, ". . . We have a law, and according to our law He ought to die, because He made Himself the Son of God" (John 19:7). Here was the implication behind this sin of envy.

But with the implication there is the application. When people accept the deity of Jesus Christ they are committed to a manner of response compatible with the demands of divine revelation. Writing to his son in the faith, Timothy, Paul says, "If anyone teaches otherwise and does not consent to wholesome words, even the words of our *Lord Jesus Christ*, and to the doctrine which is according to godliness, he is proud, knowing nothing, but is obsessed with disputes and arguments over words, *from which come envy . . .*" (1 Tim. 6:3–4). The application is clear: To reject the Lord Jesus Christ and the doctrine of godliness is to be proud and envious. It is a simple, but serious, matter of cause and effect.

Even more basic to this passage is the unveiling of human sin that is portrayed for us in Romans 1:28–29. Writing of the depravity of human hearts, Paul says that when men refuse to retain God in their knowledge they are given up to the fullness of envy. This is true of personal life, social life, national life, and ecclesiastical life. The hatred, jealousy, and malice evident in religious circles today is the direct result of the rejection of the deity of Jesus Christ. If he is only a man like ourselves then he is just a religious convenience or a compelling image; but if he is God then we must either own and obey him as God or we react with envy, malice, and murder in our hearts.

B. Envy Is the Rejection of the Sovereignty of Jesus Christ.

"For . . . [Pilate] knew that the chief priests had handed Him over because of envy" (15:10). The main issue on which Pilate and the religious leaders crossed swords was the sovereignty of Jesus Christ. What infuriated the chief priests and Pharisees was the fact that Pilate had presented Jesus Christ as the *King* of the Jews (see Mark 15:9; also John 18:36–37; 19:14–15). The same crowd, only a few days earlier, had chanted, ". . . Hosanna to the Son of David! 'Blessed is He who comes in the name of the LORD!' Hosanna in the highest!" When the chief priests and scribes saw the wonderful things that Christ did, and heard the children singing, ". . . 'Hosanna to the son of David!' *they were indignant*" (Matt. 21:9, 15). Even then there was a rejection of the sovereignty of Jesus Christ; but now that Pilate had confirmed the same messianic kingship, the malice and envy of these leaders knew no bounds.

Once again, an important principle underlies the reactions of the leaders and people to the declared sovereignty of Jesus Christ. Paul reminds us that there is a fundamental distinction between the fruit of the Spirit and the works of the flesh (cf. Gal. 5:22–23; 5:16–26). No one can be filled with the Spirit of God without the acknowledgment of Jesus Christ as undisputed Lord (see 1 Cor. 12:3). When the Spirit fills the life fruit appears; where there is a refusal to own the Lordship of Christ the works of the flesh are inevitable (see Gal. 5:19–21; Titus 3:3)—among them envy.

Envy, therefore, is the direct result of rejecting the deity and sovereignty of Jesus Christ. This is what we mean by the conception of the sin of envy. Let us see that this lust is never found in our hearts for, ultimately, it brings forth death (see James 1:15).

Illustration

The young lady to whom Mozart was first engaged to be married became discontented with her choice when she saw more of the world, and gave up the composer. She thought him too small in stature. When the world had begun to recognize his greatness, she explained her refusal of him by saying: "I knew nothing of the greatness of his genius. I saw only a little man." Isaiah speaks of the rejection of Christ by the world in much the say way. These are his words: "He is despised and rejected of men." But oh! how disappointed will those men be, when they shall see Him in His beauty![1]

II. The Consequence of the Sin of Envy

"For . . . [Pilate] knew that the chief priests had handed Him over because of envy" (15:10). Following this statement we read that ". . . the chief priests stirred up the crowd . . ." (15:11). The sin of envy is inflammable: it can burn like coals of fire, quickly spread like a flame, and get out of control (see Song of Sol. 8:6).

A. Envy Distorts the Sense of All True Value

". . . the chief priests stirred up the crowd, so that he should . . . release Barabbas . . ." (15:11). This is quite astonishing. Everybody in the crowd knew that Barabbas was a prisoner who had been condemned for insurrection and murder; yet so distorted was all sense of value that the people cried for the release of Barabbas and the *crucifixion* of our Lord. Think of it: Barabbas instead of Jesus, a robber instead of a giver, a sinner instead of a Savior, a killer instead of a healer, a peacebreaker instead of a peacemaker. This is how envy distorts all sense of value. Once a person is mesmerized by this green-eyed monster he will stoop to any level of sin. This is true of the unregenerate; it is also true of the regenerate. Even though born of the Spirit of God, every Christian is possessed of the old nature until the day of final redemption. Therefore, if and when the believer takes his eyes off the Master, envy can emerge in all its ugliness and maliciousness.

Illustration

The Devil was once crossing the Libyan Desert when he came upon a group of small fiends who were tempting a holy hermit. They tried him with the seductions of the flesh, they sought to sow his mind with doubts and fears, they told him that all his austerities were worth nothing. But it was all in vain. The holy man was impeccable. Then the Devil stepped forward. Addressing the imps he said, "Your methods are too crude. Permit me for one moment to make a recommendation." Going up to the hermit, he asked, "Have you heard the news? Your brother has been made Bishop of Alexandria." The fable says that "a scowl of malignant jealousy clouded the serene face of the holy man."[2]

B. Envy Destroys the Source of All True Virtue

"So [the people] cried out again, 'Crucify Him!' Then Pilate said to them, 'Why, what evil has He done?' And they cried out more exceedingly, 'Crucify Him!' . . .

Pilate, wanting to gratify the crowd, released Barabbas to them; and he delivered Jesus, after he had scourged Him, to be crucified" (15:13–15). This is the ultimate consequence of the sin of envy.

Everyone in that crowd that day knew of the *virtuous life* of the Lord Jesus; in him the mosaic of God's character was totalized. As a perfect man under the control of his Father, he manifested the fruit of the Spirit. Peter bore witness that he was ". . . the Christ, the Son of the living God" (Matt. 16:16). Pilate admitted, ". . . I find no fault in this Man" (Luke 23:4), and even the demons declared that he was ". . . the Holy One of God!" (Mark 1:24). In a word, Jesus Christ was the summation of all moral qualities, the incarnation of all virtue. Yet, in spite of all that Jesus revealed and represented of divine virtue, the people cried, "Crucify him! Crucify him!" Today, envy is still as ugly and sinful as it was on that first Good Friday. If it is found in your heart it will distort the sense of all true value and destroy the source of all true virtue.

Illustration

On a wall of a chapel in Padua, an old city in northeastern Italy, is a painting by the Renaissance artist Giotto. On it he depicted Envy with long ears that could hear every bit of news of another's success. He also gave to Envy the tongue of a serpent to poison the reputation of the one being envied. But if you look carefully at the painting you will notice that the tongue coils back and stings the eyes of the figure itself. Not only did Giotto picture Envy as being blind, but also as destroying itself with its own venomous evil. It always brings harm to the embittered person in whose heart it resides.[3]

III. The Conquest of the Sin of Envy

"For . . . [Pilate] knew that the chief priests had handed Him over because of envy" (15:10). Later on in the chapter

we read, ". . . the chief priests, . . . together with the
scribes, mocked and said among themselves, 'He saved
others; Himself He cannot save'" (15:31). Motivated by
envy, these blinded men could never have spoken words
more true or triumphant.

Throughout his ministry, Jesus taught, ". . . whoever
desires to save his life will lose it, but whoever loses his
life for My sake will save it" (Luke 9:24); and again:
". . . unless a grain of wheat falls into the ground and dies,
it remains alone; but if it dies, it produces much grain"
(John 12:24). This is the principle of life out of death. If
the Savior had come down from the cross every one of
those murderers would have been consigned to hell without grace, forgiveness, or hope. Instead, the master prayed
for them: ". . . Father, forgive them, for they do not know
what they do . . ." (Luke 23:34). In the mocking words of
the chief priests we see the very conquest of the sin of
envy. In their statement the enemies of Jesus unwittingly
implied:

A. The Saving Work of Christ

". . . He saved others; Himself He cannot save"
(15:31). The purpose for which the Lord Jesus came into
the world was to ". . . save His people from their sins"
(Matt. 1:21). During his ministry the master declared
that he was ". . . come to seek and to save that which
was lost" (Luke 19:10); and Paul later testified that ". . .
Christ Jesus came into the world to save sinners . . ." (1
Tim. 1:15). The interesting and yet inevitable consequence of the saving work of Christ is that it requires
and restores the concept of his deity. Even the enemies
of Jesus Christ had to admit that no one could forgive
sins but "God alone" (Mark 2:7). If we want to know
deliverance from the sin of envy we have to kneel at the
foot of the cross and exclaim with Thomas, the disciple,
". . . my Lord and *my God*!" (John 20:28). When Jesus
hung upon the cross he was reconciling the world to

himself (see 2 Cor. 5:19). In the mystery that no one can ever fathom, the entire Trinity was involved in that redemptive act of sinbearing. The Son of God, through the eternal Spirit, offered himself without spot to God when he hung upon that tree to make remission for our sins (see Heb. 9:14). He was made sin for us, who knew no sin, ". . . that we might become the righteousness of God in Him" (2 Cor. 5:21).

B. The Saving Word of Christ

". . . He saved others; Himself He cannot save" (15:31). This statement represents not only the work of Christ but the word of Christ. Without the work we would have no word to preach. Paul tells us that because of the cross we have a gospel. Indeed, he says, ". . . the message [the word] of the cross is foolishness to those who are perishing, but to us who are being saved it is the power of God" (1 Cor. 1:18). Peter reminds us that when this saving word is applied it becomes effective. He says: "But the word of the LORD endures forever. Now this is the word which by the gospel was preached to you. Therefore, laying aside all malice, all guile, hypocrisy, *envy*, and all evil speaking, as newborn babes, desire the pure milk of the word, that you may grow thereby, if indeed you have tasted that the Lord is gracious" (1 Peter 1:25–2:3).

If you are following the reasoning of this exposition you will notice that if the saving work of Christ requires and restores the concept of deity, then the word of Christ requires and restores the concept of sovereignty, *for when Jesus Christ is Lord his word is law*. A slave never answers back to his master; and as bondslaves of Jesus Christ we are committed to a life of total obedience. As we apply that saving word to our lives, day by day, we are given power to lay aside all malice, envying, and evil speaking so that we grow, like newborn babes, and prove the Lord to be full of grace and goodness in our lives.

Conclusion

By the wonder-working power of God, the cross of Christ has been turned into a throne of grace where sinners can find forgiveness and cleansing. The crime of all ages has now become the cure of all ages. So as we come afresh to the foot of the cross let us confess the sin of envy and hear the Spirit say, ". . . the blood of Jesus Christ . . . cleanses us from all sin" (1 John 1:7). But we must come with true repentance, with genuine faith, and with determined obedience. Only then will he be ". . . faithful and just to forgive us our sins and to cleanse us from all unrighteousness" (1 John 1:9); only then will we know victory over this insidious evil.

6

The Christ of the Cross
Isaiah 53:1–12

"He was wounded for our transgressions, He was bruised
for our iniquities; the chastisement for our peace was upon
Him, and by His stripes we are healed" (53:5).

Introduction

Two Old Testament passages describe the death of Christ
with remarkable comprehensiveness and arresting vivid-
ness. The first is Psalm 22, written over a thousand years
before Christ; the second, Isaiah 53, penned 700 years
before Jesus was born in Bethlehem. Surely, this is one of
the outstanding evidences of prophetic accuracy and infal-
libility. For those who know their Bible, there can be no
doubt that the person described in this fifty-third chapter
of Isaiah is Jesus Christ. When the Ethiopian eunuch
inquired of Philip the evangelist as to whom the prophet
Isaiah was referring, we read that ". . . Philip opened his
mouth, and beginning at this Scripture, preached Jesus to

him" (Acts 8:35). So in this chapter we are confronted with
the Man of Sorrows and the Christ of the cross.

Scholars point out that Isaiah 53 actually commences
with the thirteenth verse of chapter 52, and that the whole
section is divided into three divisions. We shall consider
each in order of sequence.

I. The Majesty of the Savior's Person

"Behold, My Servant shall deal prudently, He shall be
exalted and extolled and be very high. . . . So shall He
sprinkle many nations" (52:13, 15). The suffering Savior
is introduced to us here from heaven's viewpoint; and Calvary means little if we do not appreciate the majesty of
his person, as unveiled to us in these three verses:

A. The Majesty of His Sovereignty

"Behold, My Servant shall deal prudently, He shall
be exalted and extolled and be very high" (52:13). In
striking language these words describe our Savior's life
on earth—even unto the death on the cross. In total obedience to his Father's will, God's servant acted wisely
until his triumphant cry, "It is finished!" Therefore, God
could exalt him to the highest heaven. This is the sig-
nificance of the three stages referred to in verse 13—
"Behold, . . . He shall be exalted . . ."—at his resurrection; "and extolled"—at his ascension; ". . . and be very
high"—at his enthronement.

B. The Majesty of His Agony

". . . His visage was marred more than any man, and
His form more than the sons of men" (52:14). Isaiah is
telling us that the face of Christ was so marred that his
appearance was unlike the sons of men. This, of course,
was due to the brutalities that preceded his crucifixion

(see Matt. 26:67–68; 27:27–30). Disfigured as he was, however, there was a majesty about his agony. Indeed, never was Jesus Christ more a king than when he hung on Calvary's tree, wearing his crown of thorns!

Illustration

The death of Socrates, peacefully philosophizing with his friends, appears the most agreeable that could be wished for; that of Jesus, expiring in the midst of agonizing pains, abused, insulted, and accused by a whole nation, is the most horrible that could be feared. Socrates, in receiving the cup of poison, blessed the weeping executioner who administered it; but Jesus, in the midst of his tortures, prayed for his merciless tormentors. Yes! If the life and death of Socrates were those of a sage, the life and death of Jesus were those of a God.[1]

C. The Majesty of His Victory

"So shall He sprinkle many nations . . ." (52:15). If the word "sprinkle" be retained, then the sprinkling connotes the spiritual cleansing of the nations to be evangelized. Other commentators, however, render the verb "startle many nations." This would anticipate the day when that marred face is going to radiate with unspeakable glory, and nations will be startled. Kings will shut their mouths, and those who have ignored him will be obliged to give him audience and attention. Paul tells us that the time will come when ". . . at the name of Jesus every knee should bow, of those in heaven, and of those on earth, and of those under the earth, and that every tongue should confess that Jesus Christ is Lord, to the glory of God the Father" (Phil. 2:10–11).

II. The Mystery of the Savior's Passion

"Who has believed our report? And to whom has the arm of the LORD been revealed?" (53:1; see also vv. 2–9).

The cross of Christ has always been a mystery to the non-Christian. Christ crucified is a stumbling block to the Jews and foolishness to the Greeks (see 1 Cor. 1:23). That is why Isaiah the prophet asks, "Who has believed our report? And to whom has the arm of the LORD been revealed?" (53:1).

A. There Is a Mystery About the Life of Christ

"For He shall grow up before Him as a tender plant. . . . He is despised and rejected by men . . ." (53:2–3). From heaven's perspective, the coming of the Lord Jesus into the world was like ". . . a tender plant, and as a root out of dry ground . . ." (53:2). God the Father could look down upon the Savior and declare, ". . . This is My beloved Son, in whom I am well pleased" (Matt. 3:17). Amid the barrenness of lifeless religion and hopeless formalism, he was divine life, light, and love. Unregenerate men and women saw no beauty in him. Because of their sinful attitude they ". . . hid, as it were, [their] faces from him; . . . and . . . did not esteem him"; therefore, he was "despised and rejected" (53:2–3). John tells us that "He came to His own, and His own did not receive Him" (John 1:11). That is still true today. Our Savior is still despised and rejected of men. They see no beauty in him that they should desire him. This is a mystery, but it is also a fact of life.

B. There Is a Mystery About the Death of Christ

"Surely He has borne our griefs and carried our sorrows; . . . And [he] made His grave with the wicked . . ." (53:4, 9). If people find the life of Jesus hard to understand they are totally confounded when it comes to his death. Without the illumination of the Holy Spirit and genuine repentance, no one can understand the true meaning of Calvary. So Isaiah cries, "Who has believed our report? And to whom has the arm of the LORD been revealed?" (53:1). Yet with all its mysteriousness, the violent and vicarious death of Christ is the only answer to man's basic need. Only in the cross of Christ is there a full and free redemption.

Illustration

When repairs were made on an English abbey some years ago, an ancient stone wall was taken down. Behind it there was found a Saxon crucifix which experts estimated dated back to 1000 A.D. The main interest of that crucifix was that it did not show a pain-wracked victim on a cross, as so many do today, but a living, reigning Jesus, attired as high priest and crowned as king. His eyes, instead of being agonized by suffering or closed in death, are wide open in calm serenity and he is reaching down a hand—the hand which is "mighty to save." How eloquent is that ancient crucifix! When we get down at the foot of that cross we find that the place of death is really the place of life. When we die in his death we actually begin to live in his life and to reign with him.[2]

In matchless words the prophet unfolds to us the mystery of the Savior's passion:

1. IN THE DEATH OF CHRIST THERE IS A CURE FOR HUMAN SICKNESS

"Surely He has borne our griefs . . ." (53:4). The word "griefs" here is better translated "sicknesses" or "diseases." Whereas some people question whether or not physical sickness was included in the atonement, there is no doubt that moral sickness was borne away by our blessed Savior. We speak today of a "sick society"—and nothing could be more self-evident; but praise God, through the cross of Christ there is healing!

Illustration

When General William Booth, founder of the Salvation Army, died, his body lay in state for three days. Thousands filed by the old warrior's casket, which was flanked by wreaths sent by royalty and titled heads-of-state. His funeral was held in a vast exhibition hall in west London, England, attended by some 40,000—representing every strata of society—from royalty to the moral outcasts of a sick society, to whom he had ministered. A shabby, but neatly dressed woman, who had come early to claim an aisle seat, found herself seated next to Queen Mary. She confided to the queen that she had once been a prostitute and that the General had saved her. As the casket filed past, she placed three faded carnations on the lid—the only flowers on the casket—and she was heard to say, "He cared for the likes of us." What an epitaph for the General—and for our Lord, who not only loved us, but gave himself for us in death.

2. In the Death of Christ There Is a Comfort for Human Sorrow

"Surely He has borne, . . . our sorrows . . ."(53:4). As a man of sorrows, he was acquainted with everything that spells sadness, bereavement, and heartbreak; but through his cross he can turn sadness to gladness, desperation to jubilation. Only at Calvary is true joy to be found.

3. In the Death of Christ There Is a Cleansing of Human Sinfulness

"But He was wounded for our transgressions, He was bruised for our iniquities; the chastisement for our peace was upon Him, and by His stripes we are healed" (53:5). Here is a verse that declares the substitutionary work of Christ. Vicariously he was *pierced* for our transgressions, *bruised* for our iniquities, *chastised* for our peace, and *lacerated* for our healing. The words describe the violent and agonizing death which our Savior endured on our account so that we might be cleansed from our sins.

Illustration

A missionary, in the wilds of Africa, was telling the heathen the wonderful story of the Lord Jesus Christ. Seated in the front row was the chief. He had listened intently to all the missionary had said. As the missionary told of how Christ was nailed to the cross, the chief jumped to his feet and said, "Stop! Take him down from the cross; I belong there, not he!" Have you ever thanked him for [enduring an agonizing death] for you?[3]

4. IN THE DEATH OF CHRIST THERE IS A CONQUEST FOR HUMAN STRAYING

"All we like sheep have gone astray; we have turned, every one, to his own way; and the LORD has laid on Him the iniquity of us all" (53:6). Individually, socially, and nationally, people are straying creatures, just like silly sheep. But the Christ of the cross ". . . has come to seek and to save that which was lost" (Luke 19:10). In order to find us and to bring us back to himself, the Lord ". . . laid on Him [at immeasurable cost] the iniquity of us all" (53:6). We read that he was oppressed, afflicted, imprisoned, cut off, stricken, and entombed; yet in the face of all this suffering he was speechless, for ". . . He opened not His mouth . . ."; he was selfless, for ". . . He was led as a lamb to the slaughter . . ."; he was harmless, for he did no violence; he was sinless for there was no ". . . deceit in His mouth" (53:7, 9). Truly, he was the suffering Savior!

Illustration

In 1840 Bishop Selwyn, who was a missionary among the cannibal Maoris of New Zealand, wrote: "If I speak to a native of murder, infanticide, cannibalism, and adultery, they laugh in my face and tell me I may think these acts are bad, but they are very good for a native, and they cannot conceive any harm in them. But on the contrary when I tell them that these and other sins brought the Son of God, the great Creator of the universe, from his eternal glory to this

world to be incarnate and to be made a curse and to die—
they wish to hear more, and presently they acknowledge
themselves sinners, and say they will leave off their *sins*."[4]

III. The Ministry of Our Savior's Purpose

"Yet it pleased the LORD to bruise Him . . ." (53:10; see
also vv. 11–12). These words appear strange until they are
interpreted by all that follows. The fact is that the Lord
Jesus did not die in vain. He turned the crown of thorns
into a crown of gold, he transformed the cross into a
throne, and he changed an open tomb into an open
heaven. So flowing from his cross is a ministry of purpose
which Isaiah outlines for us in six glorious statements:

A. There Is the Purpose of Spiritual Fertility

". . . He shall see His seed . . ." (53:10). In pouring
out his soul as an offering for sin, the Lord Jesus has
become ". . . the firstborn among many brethren" (Rom.
8:29). Heaven is going to be populated by redeemed men
and women because of the victory of Calvary. As we
identify ourselves with his cross we become involved
in spiritual fertility. An Israelite was considered blessed
if he had many descendants—especially if he lived to
see them (see Gen. 48:11; Ps. 128:6). The Savior has seen
the fruit of his death; and we also can see this ministry
of fruitfulness as we ". . . work out [our] own salvation
with fear and trembling" (Phil. 2:12).

B. There Is the Purpose of Spiritual Longevity

". . . He shall prolong His days . . ." (53:10). The
Israelites considered longevity another blessing (see Ps.
91:16; Prov. 3:16). The reference here is to the endless
life of our risen Lord. He could declare, "I am He who
lives, and was dead, and behold, I am alive forever-

more . . ." (Rev. 1:18). Therefore he can say to us, "Because I live, you will live also" (John 14:19).

C. There Is the Purpose of Spiritual Prosperity

". . . the pleasure of the LORD shall prosper in His hand" (53:10). Because of Jesus' death and resurrection God will bring every purpose of his to a joyous realization. The phrase, "in his hand," refers to his mediatorial and high priestly ministry at the coming day when he shall reign as King of kings and Lord of lords. How wonderful that we can share in our Savior's prosperity through our union with him in life.

D. There Is the Purpose of Spiritual Maturity

"He shall see the travail of His soul, and be satisfied" (53:11). The Savior travailed in death to bring about the birth of his church, and he travails again in life to bring about the growth of the church. His purpose for his people is spiritual maturity (see Eph. 4:13). Once again, we can share in this ministry of our risen Lord. Paul reminds us that we can ". . . fill up . . . what is lacking in the afflictions of Christ, for the sake of His body, which is the church" (Col. 1:24).

E. There Is the Purpose of Spiritual Activity

"By His knowledge My righteous Servant shall justify many, for He shall bear their iniquities" (53:11). Because of who our Savior is, he not only imputes righteousness but imparts it. He commissions his servants to go forth and preach the good news of pardon, peace, and power (see John 20:21–23). As the child of God fulfills this mission he promises to bear our iniquities (53:11); in other words, he intercedes for us as our ever-living high priest (see Heb. 7:25).

F. There Is the Purpose of Spiritual Supremacy

"Therefore I will divide Him a portion with the great, and He shall divide the spoil with the strong . . ." (53:12). The Lord Jesus has overcome principalities and power and has now ". . . sat down at the right hand of the Majesty on high" (Heb. 1:3). He has won the victory over the world, the flesh, and the devil, and in this sense he has entered into his reward. The thrilling consequence of this is that we now share his victory here on earth, but one day in greater fullness when we reign with him in glory. Our position, then, is that we fight *from* victory, rather than *for* victory. Ours is the life of spiritual supremacy in and through our Lord Jesus Christ.

Here, then, is the sixfold ministry of our Savior's redemptive purpose. The world outside may question the validity of our gospel, but unto us who are saved it is both ". . . the power of God and the wisdom of God" (1 Cor. 1:24).

Conclusion

We have seen Isaiah's unveiling of the Christ of the cross: the majesty of his person, the mystery of his passion, and the ministry of his purpose. May God enable us not only to appreciate the agony of Good Friday, but also to appropriate the victory of Easter Sunday.

7

The Conquest of the Cross
John 20:19–23

"... the first day of the week, when the doors were shut ...
Jesus came ... and said to them, 'Peace be with you.' Now
when He had said this, He showed them His hands and
His side ..." (20:19–20).

Introduction

In a famous church in Copenhagen, Denmark there is a
statue of our Lord showing him alive with nail-pierced
hands outstretched. He is in the middle of his disciples—
six on one side, six on the other; and of that number the
apostle Paul takes the place of Judas. Visitors who pause to
look at the statue are moved deeply because they do not
see a victim—an emaciated Christ upon a cross—but rather
a risen Lord, displaying the battle scars of his triumph
over death, standing among his own, and commissioning
them to service.

It is this kind of vision that John gives us here in this
passage. When our Lord appeared to the disciples in the

upper room, following his resurrection, the first thing he did was to show them his hands and side. These scars of the Savior speak of:

I. The Savior's Personal Identity

"Then . . . Jesus came and stood in the midst, and said to them, 'Peace be with you.' Now when He had said this, He showed them His hands and His side [and Luke adds, "His feet"]. Then the disciples were glad when they saw the Lord" (20:19–20; Luke 24:40). The terrified disciples—and especially Thomas—would never have been convinced of the Savior's identity had he not shown them his hands and side (see 20:20). These wounds meant much to the group on that first Sunday evening. In short, the scars of the Savior signified:

A. The Christ of Calvary

". . . He showed them His hands and His side . . ." (20:20). While the disciples had deserted him, John (and probably Peter afar off) had witnessed the crucifixion. They had watched as their Lord and friend was nailed to the cross. They had observed as the spear was plunged into his side. They had seen him die. Now the Jesus of Calvary was standing among them in his risen power, showing them his hands and feet.

When John describes the heavenly vision he had of the Lord Jesus (see Rev. 5:6), he describes him as ". . . a lamb as though it had been slain. . . ." That phrase depicts the lamb now alive, but with the marks of Calvary.

B. The Christ of Victory

On that first Sunday evening, ". . . when the doors were shut where the disciples were assembled, for fear of the Jews, Jesus came and stood in the midst, and said to them, 'Peace be with you'" (20:19). No one but a conqueror could say such words. Indeed, twice over he declared, "Peace to you!" (20:21, 26). It was a peace that cancelled the guilt of the disciples, for they had all deserted him and fled. Yet despite their guilt Jesus said, ". . . Peace be with you" (20:19).

It was a peace that calmed their fears, for Luke records that ". . . they were terrified and frightened . . ." (Luke 24:37), and John and Mark confirm that they were full of fear; but Jesus said, ". . . Peace be with you" (John 20:19).

So he cancelled their guilt, calmed their fears, and cleared their doubts by his word of peace. He had bought ". . . peace through the blood of His cross" (Col. 1:20); now he brought peace by the power of his resurrection. He was indeed the Christ of victory.

This same Jesus stands before us in all the power of his resurrection life and speaks peace to us. We cannot mistake him because the scars are self-evident, and we cannot escape him because we need our guilt cancelled, our fears calmed, and our doubts cleared. Thank God, we can know the reality of this transforming experience because of the scars of the Savior.

Illustration

Stephen Olford recalls that his father visited a faithful preacher of the Word in Angola, West Africa, who was gravely ill. Bending over him, Frederick Olford whispered in his ear, "Where are you going?" The African brother replied, "To meet my Lord." "But how will you know him?" asked the missionary. For a moment the man's eyes brightened as he quoted the first two lines of a hymn which Mr. Olford had translated into the A-Chokwe language. "Ngana," he said, "I shall know him, I shall know him, by the print of the nails in his hands."

II. The Savior's Powerful Authority

". . . He showed them His hands and His side. . . . Then Jesus said to them again, 'Peace to you! As the Father has sent Me, I also send you'" (20:20–21). Those scars in his hands and side were the indisputable evidence of a completed mission. Throughout his ministry our Lord spoke of doing the Father's will and of finishing his work (see Luke 2:49; John 4:34; 9:4; 19:30). Because of that completed work God could raise him from the dead and honor him with a unique authority. When Jesus commissioned his disciples he could say, ". . . All authority has been given [past tense] to Me. . . . Go . . . make disciples of all the nations . . ." (Matt. 28:18–19). As the Son of God, this authority was always inherently his, but as the Son of Man he earned this authority by learning obedience through suffering—even the death of the cross. The evidence of this was the scars in his hands and side. Those scars endorsed his authority to condition, as well as commission, his disciples for service.

A. He Conditioned His Disciples for Service

". . . As the Father has sent Me, I also send you" (20:21). The disciples could never divorce those words from the wounds in the Savior's body. They knew that the scars spoke of his undeviating obedience to the Father's will. Three of them may have heard the Savior pray in the Garden of Gethsemane, ". . . Father, if it is possible, let this cup pass from Me; nevertheless, not as I will, but as You will" (Matt. 26:39). Now he says to them, ". . . As the Father has sent Me, I also send you" (20:21); or, "As I have obeyed the Father, so I expect you to obey me. As I brought myself under my Father's sovereign authority so I expect you to come under my sovereign authority. Look at my hands and side, and then do as I tell you."

Illustration

A little girl was being put to bed, and as her mother pulled the covers over her the girl asked a very pointed question, "Mommy," she said, "why are your hands so twisted, blotchy, and worn?" The mother replied, "Darling, when you were very little a dreadful thing happened one night. Our house caught fire and the first room to burn was the one in which you were lying asleep. I rushed in and found you enveloped in flames, and I tore the blankets and clothing from you. As I did this my hands were terribly burned. That is why they look like that." The little girl sat up and threw her arms around her mother, exclaiming, "You are the best Mommy in all the world! I will do anything for you."

The disciples must have felt something of this when the Lord Jesus showed them his hands and side and commissioned them for service.

B. He Commissioned His Disciples for Service

"As the Father has sent Me, I also send you" (20:21). The verb in the Greek is emphatic: "As the Father *has sent* Me." The death of the Lord Jesus did not abrogate his commission. True, one aspect of his work was over, but now a new stage of God's redemptive mission was being launched. This is why Luke opens up his Acts of the Apostles with the significant words, "The former account I made . . . of all that Jesus began both to do and teach" (Acts 1:1). Observe that word "began." Jesus was still working, but now he works by the Holy Spirit, through his apostles, and through you and me. Therefore, those words uttered some two thousand years ago are as relevant today as when they were first spoken: "As the Father has sent Me, I also send you" (20:21).

Illustration

S. D. Gordon, in one of his books, writes of a dream he had of the ascending Lord arriving back in heaven. He tells of the angelic hosts gathering around the Master and welcoming him home. Then he describes one of the archangels coming over to the triumphant Lord and saying, "Master, you did a great work when you were down there on earth, and it climaxed in that awful, mysterious cross; but, Master, who carries it on?" And Jesus turns and replies, "The handful of men that I have left down there." "But supposing they fail. Have you an alternative program?" insists the archangel. And the Lord Jesus looks back and says one word: "No."

The implications of that one word are tremendous. God has no other method than men. As we look at the cross and gaze upon those wounds, may it impel us to engage all our powers in the task of worldwide evangelism.

III. The Savior's Plentiful Sufficiency

"And when he had said this, he breathed on them, and said to them, 'Receive the Holy Spirit. If you forgive the sins of any, they are forgiven them; if you retain the sins of any, they are retained'" (20:22–23). We can never think of the scars of the Savior without thinking also of the sufficiency of the Savior. John links these two concepts together when he describes what happened on the cross. He writes in John 19:34: ". . . one of the soldiers pierced his side with a spear, and immediately blood and water came out." If blood is the symbol of Calvary then water is the symbol of Pentecost. When our Savior commissions his disciples he reminds them of both events. We read, ". . . He showed them His hands and His side . . ."—Calvary; ". . . Receive the Holy Spirit"—Pentecost (see 20:20, 22). He was in fact communicating to them resurrection life. As disciples they were already born of the Spirit— and presently they were to be endued with power from on high; but at this point he was giving them a new breath of life—a life they had never known before, the life of a new humanity which Jesus Christ now assumes in heaven as our representative. This is why there is no article in the Greek before the name "Holy Spirit." He said,

"Receive Holy Spirit," and many scholars maintain that the sentence could be rendered, "Receive a gift of the Spirit." Presently they were to receive the power of the Holy Spirit at Pentecost; here it was the communication of the risen life of Jesus—a gift that you and I receive at conversion. The whole act of breathing upon them symbolizes empowering for holy living and mighty preaching. Here was:

A. The Sufficiency for Holy Living

". . . He breathed on them, and said to them, 'Receive the Holy Spirit'" (20:22). Before there can be mighty preaching there must be holy living. We must be saints before we are servants. A study of the New Testament makes it evident that the fruit of the Spirit has more emphasis in the writings of the apostles than the gifts of the Spirit. What we are is more important than what we do. If what we are does not conform to the standards God expects of us then what we do is virtually worthless. God wants *us* before he wants our service. To him it is more important to be a devoted father and husband in the home than to be a famous preacher. It is more important to be a sweet, loving mother and wife than a conference speaker or a Bible class leader. It is more important that children be obedient and helpful than football stars on the field, or debaters in the classroom. Paul says, "[Be ye] filled with the Spirit" (Eph. 5:18), and he immediately adds instructions concerning loving husbands, submissive wives, and obedient children. Is the Holy Spirit dominant in your life? You won't know until Calvary is a reality to you. The Holy Spirit will never reign or rule where he is grieved or quenched. The only thing that will deal with the hindrances to a Spirit-filled life is a dynamic experience of the cross. Only when we are dead to sin can we be alive to God.

B. The Sufficiency for Mighty Preaching

Jesus said, "If you forgive the sins of any, they are for-given them; if you retain the sins of any, they are retained" (20:23). These words present certain inter-pretive problems, but in general the idea is clear. In making this statement our Savior was capsulizing the gospel message in all its fullness. The same idea is found in the closing chapter of Mark's gospel, where Jesus said, "Go into all the world and preach the gospel to every creature. He who believes and is baptized will be saved; but he who does not believe will be con-demned" (Mark 16:15–16).

To some people our message is one of salvation; to others, it is a message of damnation. Paul writes, ". . . we are to God the fragrance of Christ among those who are being saved and among those who are perishing. To the one we are the aroma of death to death, and to the other the aroma of life to life . . ." (2 Cor. 2:15–16). In another place he declares, ". . . the message of the cross is fool-ishness to those who are perishing, but to us who are being saved it is the power of God" (1 Cor. 1:18). God is described in Scripture as possessing the qualities of "goodness" and "severity" (see Rom. 11:22). Where people respond to the message of the gospel sins are remitted; where they reject the claims of Christ sins are retained.

Now while applications of this same principle are relevant in the disciplinary life of the church, we are majoring here primarily with our task as preachers and soul-winners in a world that desperately needs the mes-sage of forgiveness and reconciliation. To fulfill this mis-sion we must know sufficiency for holy living and mighty preaching.

When the Holy Spirit came upon the disciples at Pen-tecost they were fearless in their preaching. For example, Peter who cowered and cringed at the giggle of a girl on the night of the Savior's betrayal could now face the murderers of Jesus and declare, ". . . let all the house of Israel know assuredly that God has made this Jesus, whom you crucified, both Lord and Christ" (Acts 2:36). This is mighty preaching! No wonder people were convicted and converted on that memorable day!

Illustration

When Dr. Joseph Parker observed the fortieth anniversary of his pastorate in the City Temple of London, he declared: "Looking back upon all the checkered way, I have to say that the only preaching that has done me good is the preaching of a Savior who bore my sins in his own body on the tree; and the only preaching by which God has enabled me to do good to others is the preaching in which I have held up my Savior, not as a sublime example, but as 'the Lamb of God, which taketh away the sin of the world.' May God help every pastor to say with Paul, "God forbid that I should glory, except in the cross of our Lord Jesus Christ."[1]

Conclusion

What difference will the cross and the scars of the Savior make in your life? For those first-century disciples, it spelled out the identity, authority, and sufficiency of Jesus Christ as Lord and master. For us, there can only be one response. Isaac Watts has summed it up best:

> See, from his head, his hands, his feet,
> Sorrow and love flow mingled down;
> Did e'er such love and sorrow meet,
> Or thorns compose so rich a crown?
>
> Were the whole realm of nature mine,
> That were a present far too small;
> Love so amazing, so divine,
> Demands my soul, my life, my all.

Part

Other Special Sundays

Easter: *Jesus Is Alive*

2 Timothy 2:1–10

"Remember that Jesus Christ of the seed of David was raised from the dead according to my gospel" (2:8, KJV).

Introduction

No one can read the New Testament without observing that the passion and resurrection of our Lord Jesus Christ are the cardinal doctrines of our Christian faith. In the gospels we have the redemptive event; in the Acts we have the redemptive experience, and in the epistles we have the redemptive explanation of the death and resurrection of our Lord. The apostle Paul, in particular, majors on this theme in all of his writings, and insists that it is the ground of salvation and the goal of our sanctification and service.

A perfect example of this is the passage we have before us. Paul is dictating his final letter before he faces martyrdom. As he addresses Timothy, his son in the faith, he is determined that the young man shall not falter or fail under the pressures of preaching or of persecution; so he exhorts him to "remember that Jesus Christ of the seed of David was raised from the dead according to my gospel" (2:8). In other words, come what may, Jesus is alive! That fact alone guarantees endurance now and final conquest in the hour of death.

What Paul says to Timothy is the ultimate message for you and me. For us to know that Jesus is alive is all that really matters, for in our risen Lord we find the courage to live and the comfort to die. So as we look at our text we are presented with a threefold exhortation:

I. We Are to Remember the Fact of the Resurrection

"Remember that Jesus Christ of the seed of David was raised from the dead according to my gospel" (2:8). Here Paul is stating a fact which has the support of prophetic, historic, and dynamic evidence. So we do well, in this age of speculation and muddled thinking, to reexamine and reevaluate the evidence before us.

A. There Is the Fact of the Prophetic Evidence

"Remember that Jesus Christ *of the seed of David* was raised from the dead . . ." (2:8). The phrase, "of the seed of David" shifts our focus back to the prophetic utterances of the Old Testament (2 Sam. 7:12–13; Ps. 89:28; 132:17, etc.). The coming of the Lord Jesus into this world to die upon the cross and to rise again has never been a surprise to those who have understood the Scriptures. Paul could say: "Christ died for our sins *according to the Scriptures*; and . . . He was buried, and . . . He rose again the third day *according to the Scriptures*" (1 Cor. 15:3, 4).

Amplification

Show that the Old Testament Scriptures—the Law, the Psalms, and the Prophets—speak of the death and resurrection of Christ (see Gen. 3:15; Ps. 16:10–11; Ps. 22; Isa. 53, etc.).

B. There Is the Fact of the Historic Evidence

"Remember that Jesus Christ of the seed of David was raised from the dead . . ." (2 Tim. 2:8). The four gospels are united in their testimony that Jesus Christ rose from the dead. You only have to read the closing chapters of each of the evangelists to see this documented. In the Acts, the apostles are likewise united in their testimony to the resurrection of the Savior, for we read: "And with great power gave the apostles witness of the resurrection of the Lord Jesus: and great grace was upon them all" (Acts 4:33, KJV).

Amplification

Show that Paul had historic facts on which to build his doctrine of the resurrection (see 1 Cor. 15:1–11, 20).

C. There Is the Fact of the Dynamic Evidence

"Remember that Jesus Christ of the seed of David was raised from the dead according to my gospel" (2:8). The text is better rendered: "Remember that Jesus Christ is *risen from the dead*." Paul was not only concerned with the event as it occurred at a point in time, but also with the evidence of the risen life of Christ in his own experience. So he speaks of this mighty fact as "my gospel," and the more we read his testimony in the Acts and the epistles, the more we become impressed with the dynamic influence this truth had upon his life.

Illustration

Use the repeated story of Paul's conversion (Acts 9:1–9; 22:6–11; 26:13–16; see also 1 Cor. 15:8).

II. We Are to Consider the Force of the Resurrection

"Remember that Jesus Christ of the seed of David was raised from the dead according to my gospel" (2:8). These words constitute the basis of a threefold encouragement which Paul gives us in this passage. Addressing his son in the faith, and Christian men and women throughout the centuries, he says: "Be strong in the grace that is in Christ Jesus" (2:1). In these words he implied a supernatural enablement to stand, strive, and serve for Christ.

A. As Christians, We Have the Power to Stand for Christ

"Thou therefore endure hardness, as a good soldier of Jesus Christ. No man that warreth entangleth himself with the affairs of this life; that he may please him who hath chosen him to be a soldier" (2:3–4). As Christians, we are engaged in a battle with the world, the flesh, and the devil. So Paul says, "Endure hardness, as a good soldier of Jesus Christ," or more literally, "Take your share of suffering" (RSV). But tough as the battle is, we are to withstand the enemy, "and having done all, to stand." The armor and weapons which God supplies make no provision for retreat or defeat. We must remember that "we are more than conquerors through him that loved us" (Rom. 8:37).

Amplification
Show that dedication, in the Christian warfare, demands freedom from all entanglements of this life.

B. As Christians, We Have the Power to Strive for Christ

"And if a man also strive for masteries, yet is he not crowned, except he strive lawfully" (2 Tim. 2:5). As Christians, we have a race to run, a course to finish. So

Paul turns our thoughts from the scene of the battle to the Olympic arena. He points out that for a contestant to qualify, as well as to win a race, he must adhere to the rules of the Olympic games. There are scholars who tell us that Paul includes here the idea of correct "running style," as well as the actual rules of running. So the challenge is not only to wholehearted devotion, as in the case of a soldier, but also wholehearted obedience to the rules of the game.

Illustration

Show from athletic events, the importance of the rules in any sport.

C. As Christians, We Have the Power to Serve for Christ

"The husbandman that laboureth must be first partaker of the fruits" (2:6). As Christians, we have a job to do, and that calls for faithfulness. Here Paul uses the imagery of the orchard. The fruit farmer must dig the ground, sow the seed, water the earth, and prune the trees—but ultimately he must exercise faith. If a farmer has no faith he may as well quit farming.

In a similar way, we must show our faithfulness in all our service for the Lord Jesus Christ. Only then shall we bear fruit that glorifies the Father (John 15:1–8).

Amplification

Show that all service calls for faithfulness, in the light of the judgment seat of Christ. There the words of commendation will be, "Well done, good and faithful servant" (Matt. 25:23).

III. We Are to Deliver the Faith of the Resurrection

"Remember that Jesus Christ of the seed of David was raised from the dead according to my gospel: wherein I suf-

fer trouble, as an evil doer, even unto bonds; but the word of
God is not bound. Therefore I endure all things for the elect's
sakes" (2 Tim. 2:8–10). If we have been convinced of the fact
and the force of the resurrection we cannot be silent about
the faith. This is what Paul is telling us in the closing verses
of this paragraph. Because the Lord Jesus Christ was a living reality to him, Paul was prepared to preach the gospel,
whatever the cost and wherever the call. This is precisely
what he wanted Timothy to do, and what he wants us to do.

A. We Must Preach the Gospel Whatever the Cost

"Wherein I suffer trouble, as an evil doer, even unto
bonds; but the word of God is not bound" (2:9). Paul takes
pains to tell Timothy—and his readers throughout the
centuries—that the communication of their faith involves
real effort and personal sacrifice. Indeed, he points out
that in the course of preaching the gospel he was accused
of being an evildoer and was punished accordingly.
Indeed, the word "evildoer" really means "a criminal"
or "a malefactor." It is the same term used for the malefac-
tors who were crucified with Jesus (Luke 23:32, 39). There
is a searching suggestion here that to be involved in making known the message of the risen Christ is to suffer persecution with our Lord and Savior Jesus Christ. If we are
not prepared to share his shame then we are not worthy
to sit with him on the throne (2 Tim. 2:11–12).

Illustration

Show the costliness of preaching Christ in many parts of
the world today. It is a statistical fact that more people
have laid down their lives for Christ in this century than in
all the other centuries of church history.

B. We Must Preach the Gospel Wherever the Call

"Therefore I endure all things for the elect's sakes,
that they may also obtain the salvation which is in

Christ Jesus with eternal glory" (2:10). God is calling
out a people for his name. In his sovereign foreknowl-
edge he has elected those who are "ordained unto eternal life," and this is precisely what Paul has in mind in
this verse. He talks about the elect who have yet to
obtain salvation in Christ Jesus. The elect are scattered
all over the world, and so must be searched out with
the word of the gospel. Indeed, the fact that we do not
know where the elect are to be found constitutes one of
the most powerful incentives to fulfill the mandate of
the master, to "preach the gospel to every creature"
(Mark 16:15). We cannot afford to choose our own mission field; we must go wherever God sends us.

Illustration

Show how God calls his servants to specific spheres of
service.

Conclusion

So the message of Easter is Jesus is alive! This is the fact
that we must see, this is the force that we must seek, and
this is the faith that we must share. God enable us to enter
into the true meaning of the *living Jesus!*

9

Mother's Day:
Faith of Our Mothers
2 Timothy 1:1–5; 3:12–17

"I call to remembrance the unfeigned faith . . . which dwelt first in thy grandmother Lois, and thy mother Eunice" (1:5).

Introduction

Writing of Timothy, his son in the faith, Paul could say with unaffected frankness, "I have no man like-minded" (Phil. 2:20), or, as another translation reads, "There is no one like Timothy." What in Timothy justified such a commendation? Part of the answer is given in our text; recalling Timothy's sterling qualities, Paul singles out his "unfeigned faith" for special mention (2 Tim. 1:5), and then immediately affirms that this faith dwelt first in Timothy's grandmother Lois, and in his mother Eunice. Paul implies that but for the faith found in Lois and Eunice it is unlikely that there would have been any faith found in Timothy! We have here, then, the faith of three generations—Lois, Eunice, and Timothy. What a commentary this is on the faith of our mothers!

I. A Mother's Faith Is Convictional

"The unfeigned faith . . . which dwelt first in thy grandmother Lois, and thy mother Eunice" (1:5). A careful study of Acts 16:1, together with 2 Timothy 1 and 2 Timothy 3:14, makes it plain that these two women enjoyed a faith in God through our Lord Jesus Christ which was both scriptural and saving, a good example of the nature of convictional faith.

A. It Is a Faith Which Is Scripturally Sound

Both these mothers knew "the holy scriptures, which are able to make . . . wise unto salvation" (2 Tim. 3:15, KJV). They could have never taught Timothy these sacred writings if they had not been acquainted with them personally. Such study of the Holy Scriptures had begotten in them a God-centered faith. And this is how it always is, for the Bible says, "Faith cometh by hearing, and hearing by the word of God" (Rom. 10:17). Above tradition and secular literature, they prized most highly the final authority in all matters of faith and practice, namely the Holy Scriptures.

Amplification

Show how important it is for a wife and mother to live in the Scriptures day by day. Explain the necessity of a daily quiet time.

B. It Is a Faith Which Is Savingly Sure

They taught Timothy "the holy scriptures which are able to make . . . wise unto salvation through faith which is in Christ Jesus" (2 Tim. 3:15). From Acts 16:1 it appears that both Timothy's mother and grandmother were introduced to a saving knowledge of Jesus Christ on Paul's second missionary journey. Eunice is there described as a Jewish woman who "believed." Their background of scriptural knowledge had wonderfully prepared them for the message of salvation through Paul the apostle.

Here, then, were two mothers who had a convictional faith, grounded in the Word of God and related to Jesus Christ as Savior and Lord. Nothing is needed more in our land today than women who have this quality of faith.

Illustration

For example, an African chief wanted to know the secret of Britain's greatness. Queen Victoria, holding a Bible in her hand, said, "Tell the chief that this book, the Bible, is the secret of our greatness."

II. A Mother's Faith Is Communicable

"Call to remembrance the unfeigned faith . . . which dwelt first in thy grandmother Lois, and thy mother Eunice. . . . But continue thou in the things which thou hast learned and hast been assured of, knowing of whom thou hast learned them" (1:5; 3:14). There is no one who can communicate the deep things of life on a daily basis like a godly mother. The father certainly has a responsibility of leadership, both by way of example and instruction, but invariably it is the mother who makes the deepest impression on a child, especially in the years of infancy.

A. Faith Is Communicated by Personal Education

"But continue thou in the things which thou hast learned and hast been assured of, knowing of whom thou hast learned them" (3:14). From his earliest days,

Timothy was taught the Holy Scriptures. This sense of duty to communicate the Word of God was rooted in God's instruction to his ancient people. In other words, the devout Israelite taught his children because Jehovah commanded him to do so.

Amplification

Show how religious education is not only the privilege, but the responsibility of every godly home (see Deut. 4:9–10; 6:6–15; 11:18–21; Prov. 6:20, 21; 7:1–3; 22:6).

B. Faith Is Communicated by Practical Demonstration

"But continue thou in the things which thou hast learned and hast been *assured of*, knowing of whom thou hast learned them" (3:14). While Paul undoubtedly includes himself in that expression, "knowing of whom thou hast learned them," his primary thought is that of Lois and Eunice. Timothy had seen something in their lives that demonstrated the reality of the faith they taught.

Amplification

Expound Ephesians 6:4 and Colossians 3:21.

Illustration

John Newton, in his most profligate days, could never forget his mother at whose knees he had learned to pray, but who was taken to heaven when he was only eight years old. "My mother's God, the God of mercy, have mercy upon me!" was often his agonizing prayer when in danger or in trouble. That prayer was gloriously answered—not only in Newton's life, but also in his subsequent ministry.

In another family, such was the impression that Susannah Wesley made on her son, John, that she has been called "The mother of Methodism."

III. A Mother's Faith Is Commendable

Paul says, "I call to remembrance the unfeigned faith . . . which dwelt first in thy grandmother Lois, and thy mother Eunice" (1:5). Some have suggested that Paul actually stayed in Timothy's home during the second missionary journey. If that was so, then quite obviously he was impressed with what he saw in the lives of both Lois and Eunice. While it was his privilege to bring to consummation their faith in the Lord Jesus Christ as Savior and master, he could never forget the religious faith and piety which were already evident in their lives.

A. The Lasting Influence of a Mother's Faith

"I call to remembrance the unfeigned faith . . . which dwelt first in thy grandmother Lois, and thy mother, Eunice" (1:5). Has it ever occurred to you that the most priceless treasure a man or woman can have is *faith*? The world may cry, "What is a man without money?" but the Christian replies, "What is a man without faith?" Remember, the only thing by which all the heroes of the Old Testament are remembered, in the eleventh chapter of Hebrews, is their faith. Like a refrain, we read it in verse after verse: "By faith Abel" (Heb. 11:4), "By faith Enoch" (11:5), "Through faith . . . Sara" (11:11), "By faith . . . Rahab" (11:31), and so on.

Illustration

Show the preciousness and power of a living faith.

F. B. Meyer once said: "It is not the quantity of faith, but the quality of faith, that is important. A grain of mustard seed and a pellet of dust are similar in appearance, but the difference is immense. The one has no life burning at the heart of it, while the other contains life as God kindled it. Faith that has in it the principle of life is a faith with God in it."

B. The Living Relevance of a Mother's Faith

"I call to remembrance the *unfeigned* faith that . . . dwelt first in thy grandmother Lois, and thy mother Eunice" (2 Tim. 1:5). Times may change and fashions may alter, but mothers are never out of date! There is a living relevance in a mother's faith because no one in all the world adapts herself to the day in which she lives like a mother with her little children. Someone has said that "a space-age mother needs to keep her feet on the ground and her heart in the heavens. The man on the moon will never replace the man in the home with a dedicated wife working with him to raise a Christian family."

Illustration

William McKinley, as a lawyer, congressman, Governor of Ohio, and President of the United States, kept in touch with his mother every day. When he didn't see her, he wrote or telegraphed. In mid-October of 1897, he quietly left the White House and took a train to Canton just so he could walk to church with her again. When she became ill, he arranged to have a special train standing by at full steam, ready to take him to her bedside. Then one night she did call for him. Immediately he wired, "Tell mother I'll be there." Mrs. McKinley died December 12, 1897, in the arms of her 54-year-old son. Her gentle, Christian virtues helped mold the President's character, for when he was gunned down in Buffalo, New York, about four years later, he showed no bitterness toward his assassin. With Christian courage he said, "God's will be done." Before he died, he asked to hear once again the hymn, "Nearer, My God, to Thee," which his mother had taught him.[1]

Conclusion

Let us see to it that the mothers of our generation know a faith in God's Word and in his Son Jesus Christ which

is convictional, communicable, and commendable. Only
then can we sing:

> Faith of our mothers! living still,
> In spite of dark'ning days of doubt;
> O how our beings glow and thrill,
> When that word "faith" is sounded out!
>
> Faith of our mothers! gift of grace,
> Born of the Spirit from on high;
> Nourished by Scripture, strong to face,
> Forces of evil when they're nigh.
>
> Faith of our mothers! Lord preserve,
> This priceless treasure to us all;
> That through our families we may serve
> Duty or danger when they call.
>
> So bless our mothers! every one,
> Bless them for holy faith and love;
> God bless them now for work well done,
> Then honor them in realms above.
>
> (Tune: Faith of Our Fathers)

10

Labor Day Sunday: *Divine Service*

John 9:1–7

"I must work the works of Him who sent Me while it is day; the night is coming when no one can work" (9:4).

Introduction

Christians will never come to regard the work of God with any sense of importance and imperativeness until they learn that it is *divine service*. In its origin, operation, and consummation, the work of God is divine. Jesus could say, ". . . my Father has been working until now, and I have been working" (John 5:17); and Paul could add, "we . . .[are] workers together with Him . . ." (2 Cor. 6:1). But the greatest statement on this subject is right here in our text. The Greek has it, "*We* must work the works of Him who sent Me . . ." (9:4). Obviously, the Lord Jesus was identifying himself with his disciples. He is showing them that association with him in the doing of the work of God

89

is nothing less than divine service. What dignity, liberty, and urgency this brings into our Christian service, wherever it is, at home and abroad! The master was teaching:

I. The Divine Obligation to Service

"[We] *must* work the works of Him who sent Me . . ." (9:4). The person who says that he has no sense of obligation to serve God is a person who has never received the divine nature. ". . . faith by itself, if it does not have works, is dead," says James (James 2:17). Paul declares: ". . . we are His workmanship, created in Christ Jesus for good works, which God prepared beforehand that we should walk in them" (Eph. 2:10). In other words, to know a living faith in Christ and to share that divine nature is to be linked with the divine activity of God in time and in eternity. This divine obligation expresses itself in a lifelong sense of:

A. Responsibility to God

"[We] must work the works of Him who sent Me . . ." (9:4). Service for the Lord Jesus was both important and imperative. As a *Son*, he could say, ". . . I must be about My Father's business" (Luke 2:49). Though subject to his earthly parents, he was supremely responsible to his God and Father. The writer to the Hebrews reminds us, "though He was a Son, yet He learned obedience by the things which He suffered" (Heb. 5:8). Oh, that a sense of imperative obedience might come into our lives as sons of God! This is his purpose in conferring upon us the high privilege of sonship.

Illustration

In India, as in other countries that were under British rule, the letters O.H.M.S. (On His Majesty's Service) used to be printed on official documents and envelopes. In those days, the son of devoted missionaries in the district of West Godavari was asked by relatives in Canada what the letters stood for. He explained that in his prayers with his parents he used to express his desire in the following way: "Lord, I'm just like a government letter. No matter what becomes blurred or defaced on me, please keep the letters—O.H.M.S.—on me clear."[1]

As a *Savior* he predicted: ". . . the Son of Man [must] be lifted up, that whoever believes in Him should not perish but have eternal life" (John 3:14–15). There was a divine imperative in every aspect of his redemptive work. There was no question of holding back at any point, even though it meant the death of the cross (see Luke 22:42). There is a sense in which God calls us to share the redemptive activity of our Lord. This does not include the unique and final work which he accomplished at Calvary, but it does involve the practical outworking of the ministry of the cross in terms of everyday living and serving. Paul speaks of it as filling up that which is lacking in the affliction of Christ, for his body's sake (see Col. 1:24). Have we accepted this imperative in our Christian service?

As a *Servant*, God's perfect bondslave, he made himself of no reputation, renounced all rights, and was totally dependent on God for the fulfilling of his perfect will.

The apostle Paul is an outstanding example of identification with Christ in this sense of responsibility in Christian service. He was ever under a sense of burden to fulfill the will of God. He could say, ". . . woe is me if I do not preach the gospel!" (1 Cor. 9:16). Evangelism was the burden of John Knox who cried, "Give me Scotland or I die." It was the declaration of John Wesley, "The world is my parish." It is the sob of parents, weeping over their prodigal children.

B. Accountability to God

"[We] must work the works of Him who sent Me . . ."
(9:4). The Savior's awareness of being sent made him
ever accountable to God. He never spoke without the
words being given him of God (see John 8:28). He never
did anything without heaven's permission (see John
5:19, 30).

We, too, are accountable to God for our words and
actions; we cannot afford to act independently of God
for a single moment. It is because we have lost this sense
of eternity that we have become indolent and negligent
in our Christian service. We have forgotten that if we
are saved then we are sent. Our very oneness with Christ
in salvation makes us one with him in service.

Illustration

Many years ago, Joe Creeson, of the *Louisville Courier
Journal*, knew a man who had the job of polishing locomo-
tives. Several men worked at the job, but this one worked
longer, harder, and produced better results. One day Creeson asked him, "Why do you work so hard? Why does the
engine have to be so shiny?" And the old man said, "Joe, I
got the glory." He'd been converted. For that old man, it
was an act of divine worship to take an old locomotive that
could barely puff down the tracks and make certain it was
clean and shiny. He knew God had given him his body, his
strength, and his job. Therefore, he wanted to honor God
through the way he worked.[2]

II. The Divine Objective in Service

"[We] must work the works of Him who sent Me . . ."
(9:4). The ultimate objective of divine service is not only
unfolded throughout this gospel, but is dramatically illustrated in the very context of this chapter. It implies:

A. The Personal Receiving of Christ

In chapter 6 of John the Lord Jesus says: ". . . This is the work of God, that you believe in Him whom He sent" (v. 29); and in chapter 1, verse 12, the apostle defines what is involved in believing. He writes: ". . . as many as received Him, to them He gave the right to become children of God, even to those who believe in His name." No one has the right to engage in so-called service for God until they have personally received Christ. Thousands of people are involved in religious activism who know nothing of the indwelling life of Jesus, but, according to the master, this is the first essential for a life of service.

Before Jesus opened the eyes of the blind man to fulfill the work of God (see John 9:4–7), he spat on the ground, mixed clay with his own saliva, then applied it to the man's eyes. And we read that he "came back seeing" (9:7). The admixture of the divine spittle with earthly clay provides one of the most dramatic object lessons in the New Testament concerning the indwelt life. Before we can open the eyes of blind men and women we must know what it is to be ". . . partakers of the divine nature . . ." (2 Peter 1:4). Any service done in a humanitarian way may be impressive, but it is virtually worthless in the sight of God. This explains why there is such dearth and death in our churches today.

B. The Personal Revealing of Christ

"Most assuredly, I say to you, he who believes in Me, the works that I do he will do also; and greater works than these he will do, because I go to My Father" (John 14:12). Observe that the supreme work that Jesus came to do was that of revealing his Father. He had just said to Philip, ". . . He who has seen Me has seen the Father . . ." (14:9).

Now see this illustrated in the same story that we are considering. The next time Jesus encountered this man, following his miraculous healing, was to reveal himself to him (see 9:35–38): "Jesus heard that they had cast him out; and when He had found him, He said to him, 'Do you believe in the Son of God?' He answered and said, 'Who is He, Lord, that I may believe in Him?' And Jesus said to him, 'You have both seen Him and it is He who is talking with you.' Then he said, 'Lord, I believe!' And he worshiped Him."

Needless to say, we cannot reveal Christ until we have received Christ; but if there is a genuine experience of the indwelling Savior, the supreme work of every Christian is to reveal Christ—consciously, conspicuously, and continually in every area of life.

Illustration

The children were arranging the figures of Mary, Joseph, and the Christ Child in the little manger scene. They lighted two candles and carefully tried them in various positions until the light fell exactly where they wanted it. One child excitedly said, "Be sure that Jesus shows!" How wonderful if this thought were uppermost in our daily lives—"Be sure that Jesus shows." Like the candles, we can direct attention to Christ in our daily actions and proclaim to our neighbors that we are genuine Christians.[3]

In practical terms, we reveal Christ by:

1. The Method of Evangelization

"Go therefore and make disciples of all the nations . . ." (Matt. 28:19). The work of evangelization is confronting men and women with the risen Christ. The divine method of doing this is not through impersonal organization, but through personal evangelism. The Holy Spirit had to come upon those early disciples with ". . . power from on high" (Luke 24:49) in order for them to be witnesses to the uttermost part of the earth. We have reversed the order and have tried to impress the world with our church programs, attractive publicity, and modern techniques; but our text contradicts this kind of approach and makes it evident that the only effective means of winning the world is through men and women in whom Jesus Christ resides and in whom he is gloriously revealed in all his attractiveness and power to save.

Illustration

In *The Life of John William Fletcher*, Robert Cox wrote, "He frequently preached at the French church in Dublin, which was attended by the descendants of the persecuted Huguenots. Among his hearers were some persons who were totally unacquainted with the French language. Being questioned respecting the motives for their attendance, they instantly replied, 'We went to *look* at him, for heaven seemed to beam from his countenance.'" God derives great pleasure from seeing Christ revealed in saints below.[4]

2. THE MESSAGE OF IDENTIFICATION

"Go therefore and make disciples of all the nations, baptizing them in the name of the Father and of the Son and of the Holy Spirit" (Matt. 28:19). The message of identification rules out all that is of self, and reveals all that is of Christ. When you get a group of people who are living on this basis you have a real church. Fellowship, in the New Testament sense of the word, is the shared resurrection life of Jesus, and such a life can never be enjoyed without the experience of death and burial to self.

3. THE MINISTRY OF EDUCATION

"Go . . . . teaching them to observe all things that I have commanded you . . ." (Matt. 28:19–20). Unless people have really come face to face with Christ through evangelization and identification it is futile to try and teach them the deep things of God; it makes no impression on them whatsoever. It was only when the Savior's disciples were wholly identified with him that he could pray for them: "Sanctify them by Your truth. Your word is truth" (John 17:17). Our ultimate aim should be to warn every man and teach every man ". . . in all wisdom, that we may present every man perfect in Christ Jesus" (Col. 1:28). Such education is designed to reveal Christ in all his fullness and glory.

God has no other reason for leaving us on earth, following our conversion, unless it is to serve him in the winning of souls. Our spheres of activity may be varied, but the objective is the same. For some, the pulpit may be the home; for others, an office in the city, the university campus, or missionary service overseas. Ultimately, there is only one goal: the completion of the body of Christ through every-member evangelism. How we earn our bread and butter is secondary; the primary call is the same as that which motivated our blessed Savior when he said, "I must work the works of Him who sent Me . . ." (9:4).

III. The Divine Opportunity of Service

"[We] must work the works of Him who sent Me *while it is day . . .*" (9:4). A sense of urgency characterized our Lord in everything he said and did. By his life he taught and demonstrated two important principles in regard to the matter of opportunity:

A. All Time Must Be Redemptively Utilized

"[We] must work the works of Him who sent Me, while it is day . . ." (9:4). Jesus worked to a timetable and therefore never wasted a moment; he was never caught off guard. Recall the occasion when his mother prematurely asked him to perform a miracle at the wedding of Cana. He replied with gentle insistence: ". . .

Woman, what does your concern have to do with Me? My hour has not yet come" (John 2:4). Later, at the end of his ministry, he could say, ". . . for this purpose I came to this hour" (John 12:27); and still again: ". . . The hour has come . . ." (John 12:23).

No one has ever been great or useful, in the highest sense, who has not regarded time in a similar manner. Have you heard these words?

> When as a child I laughed and wept,
> > Time crept;
> When as a youth I dreamt and talked,
> > Time walked;
> When I became a full-grown man,
> > Time ran;
> When older still I daily grew,
> > Time flew;
> Soon shall I find in traveling on,
> > Time gone . . .[5]

May God ". . . teach us to number our days, that we may gain a heart of wisdom" (Ps. 90:12); or to put it in the language of the New Testament: "redeeming the time, because the days are evil" (Eph. 5:16).

Amplification

Everyone receives an equal supply of time. The only difference between us is in the way we spend it. Each week brings us 168 golden hours. We spend approximately 28 hours for eating and personal duties. We spend approximately 40 to 50 hours for earning a living. We have 30 to 40 hours left to spend just as we wish. But how do we spend them? How many hours for recreation? How many hours for family fellowship? How many hours for the regular worship of God? How many hours for personal service in the name of Christ? Will a man rob God? He can; and he does. Perhaps we may be very busy with good things, yet be too busy for the best things. The great question is: Have we made wise use of our time as good stewards of Christ?

B. All Talents Must Be Redemptively Exercised

"[We] must work the works of Him who sent Me . . ."
(9:4). The Lord Jesus gave his all, and so must we. The
language of the apostle Paul must ever characterize our
availability for God: "So, as much as is in me, I am ready
to preach the gospel . . ." (Rom. 1:15). Or to put it in the
words of a lovely chorus:

> All my days, and all my hours;
> All my will, and all my powers;
> All the passion of my soul,
> Not a fragment but the whole
> Shall be Thine, dear Lord,
> Shall be Thine, dear Lord.[6]
>
> Edward H. Joy

Conclusion

God has given us today. Tomorrow may never come.
One of the most solemn realizations that can come to a
Christian is that he can miss God's day of opportunity.
Paul was addressing Christians when he wrote: ". . . Behold,
now is the accepted time; behold, *now* is the day of salva-
tion" (2 Cor. 6:2).

11

Missions Sunday:
Winged Feet
Isaiah 52:1–12

"How beautiful upon the mountains are the feet of him who brings good news, who proclaims peace, who brings glad tidings of good things, who proclaims salvation, who says to Zion, 'Your God reigns!'" (52:7).

Introduction

To understand prophetic writings we must recognize that they have a literal as well as spiritual sense. The words before us in their primary meaning refer to the news of deliverance which the heralds proclaimed to Jerusalem when King Cyrus permitted the captive Jews to return from Babylon to their native country. But it is equally true that these words relate to the preaching of the gospel in this dispensation of grace (see Rom. 10:13–15).

The picture which the Holy Spirit gives the prophet Isaiah is that of couriers running and skipping upon the

mountains as they hurry to the city of Jerusalem to declare
their good news. As Franz Delitzsch puts it: "The excla-
mation, 'How lovely,' does not refer to the lovely sound
of their footsteps, but to the lovely appearance presented
by their feet which spring over the mountains with all the
swiftness of gazelles. Their feet look as if they had *wings*
because they are the messengers of good tidings of joy."
These winged feet speak of:

I. The Universality of the Divine Message

"How beautiful upon the mountains are the feet of him
who brings good news, who proclaims peace, who brings
glad tidings of good things, who proclaims salvation, who
says to Zion, 'Your God reigns!'" (52:7). The very concept
of feet with wings suggests universality of movement.
God's message of good news is for all the world for all the
ages. Observe that:

A. God's Message Is Universal in Its Nature

". . . good news, . . . peace, . . . good things, . . . salvation, . . . who says to Zion, 'Your God reigns!'" (52:7).
Man cannot achieve his true humanity without God.
Therefore, wherever he is found, he is basically hungry
and thirsty for the only message that will relate him to
God through faith in Christ. This is the universal character of the gospel. Geographical distances, language barriers, and cultural distinctions, make no difference to the
appeal of the gospel. Black and yellow, red and white,
are all candidates for the message of the living God. That
message, very simply, is that God reigns, and through
Christ offers the good news of redeeming grace, or what
Isaiah calls the good news of peace (52:7). Through the
cross of his Son God has made possible a basis of reconciliation whereby every sinner can know pardon and
peace, if he truly repents and believes the gospel.

But God also offers *renewing grace,* for the text tells of "tidings of good" (52:7). He not only forgives and cleanses the sinner, but transforms him into the image of his own Son. No one becomes truly "good" until he becomes united to Christ. And with that renewing grace there is *releasing grace*—"tidings of . . . salvation" (52:7). This is complete deliverance from sin, self, and Satan.

What a message for winged feet to carry to all the world!

Illustration

When Jonathan Goforth first arrived in China, an old, experienced missionary gave him this advice: "Do not attempt to speak of Jesus the first time you preach to a heathen audience. The Chinese have a prejudice against the name of Jesus. Confine your efforts to demolishing the false gods, and if you have a second opportunity you may bring in Jesus." Later that evening, Goforth shared with his wife the advice that had been given him, and with hot emphasis he added, "NEVER, NEVER, NEVER! The gospel which saved the down-and-outs in the slums of Toronto is the same gospel that must save Chinese sinners." Years later more than one missionary came to Jonathan Goforth and asked what the secret of power was to get men out of the depths of their sin. He replied, "I simply believe and teach God's Word. Some have said you cannot preach to a proud Confucian scholar the same as to the common crowd," but he added, "There is no royal road to God. Rich or poor, Chinese or Canadians, educated or ignorant, all are sinners and therefore must come to the same Savior by the same road."[1]

B. God's Message Is Universal in Its Need

"How beautiful upon the mountains are the feet of him who brings good news . . ." (52:7). The Chaldeans who so grievously oppressed their Jewish captives may justly represent the bitter and tyrannical dominion of sin and Satan; and Cyrus, who without fee or reward liberated them from their bondage, may be considered as the agent and representative of God (52:3). Just as the messengers would remind the Jews that Cyrus had wrought deliverance for them, so preachers today declare that Christ has come to set the captives free and to give deliverance to all who are bound. How needed is this message of redeeming love, renewing life, and releasing power in our world at this hour!

It is evident from this passage that before the good news arrived there was nothing but bad news. Before the message of peace was proclaimed there was nothing but unrest and turmoil. None of the captives could say, "My God reigns." We shall never know anything of winged feet until we sense this universal need.

Illustration

Robert Moffatt, a missionary on furlough in England, was telling about the dark continent of Africa. In the audience that day was a young Scot named David Livingstone. He was studying to be a doctor and had decided to give his life to the service of God, but where and how he was not sure. As he listened to Dr. Moffatt's story, he heard the missionary say, "There is a vast plain to the north where I have sometimes seen, in the morning sun, *the smoke of a thousand villages* where no missionary has ever been." Livingstone never forgot those words—"the smoke of a thousand villages." Afterwards he went to Dr. Moffatt and asked, "Would I do for Africa?" That moment constituted David Livingstone's great decision. It was not only the nature of the gospel but also the need for the gospel which won his heart and life.

II. The Urgency of the Divine Mission

"How beautiful upon the mountains are the feet of him who brings good news . . ." (52:7). It is one thing to know the gospel, but quite another to preach it to every creature. It is just at this point that the Church has failed. She has the message but not the sense of mission.

Isaiah does not speak here of the beauty of the eyes, or of
the lips, or of the hands of these heralds of good news. On
the contrary, he speaks of the beauty of the feet. The meaning is clear. To see the need, to preach the Word, and to
serve the Lord are inconsequential if we are not in the
place of God's appointment. We need winged feet to take
us to the fields of his choosing. Winged feet speak of:

A. Mobility in Service

". . . the feet . . .[that bring] good news . . ." (52:7).
The Bible is the story of God in action; he never slum-
bers nor sleeps (see Ps. 121:4; John 5:17). It was likewise said of the master that he was ". . . a Prophet
mighty in deed and word before God and all the people"
(Luke 24:19). The ceaseless activity of the Savior was
demonstrated in that he ". . . went about doing good
and healing all who were oppressed by the devil. . . ."
(Acts 10:38).

Before Pentecost God promised his heralds that the
Holy Spirit would come upon them in order that they
might be witnesses to him in Jerusalem, Judea, Samaria,
and unto the uttermost part of the earth (see Acts 1:8).
The whole idea of the Great Commission is that of
mobility and action (See Mark 16:15). Later, when Paul
argued for the resurrection and the livingness of our
Lord, he concluded that classic passage in 1 Corinthi-
ans 15 by saying, "Therefore, my beloved brethren, be
steadfast, immovable, *always abounding* in the work of
the Lord, knowing that your labor is not in vain in the
Lord" (v. 58). No one can share the resurrection life of
Christ without having winged feet. Ask yourself, are
you active for Jesus Christ?

Illustration

A minister was once asked by a friend how many members he had in his church. "One thousand," the preacher
replied. "Really?" the friend exclaimed, "and how many

of them are active?" "All of them are active," was the
response. "About two hundred are active for the Lord;
the balance are active for the devil." On which side are
you? Jesus said, "He that is not with me is against me;
and he that gathereth not with me scattereth abroad"
(Matt. 12:30). There can be no neutrality in this matter of
mobility. We are either active for the Lord or active for
the devil.

B. Rapidity in Service

". . . the feet of him who brings good news . . ." (52:7).
It is one thing to be mobile, but quite another to be fast
or swift. Isaiah gives a picture here of the beautiful
gazelle whose movements are fast and swift.

It is interesting and important to observe that all ref-
erences to living and preaching the gospel have to do
with the urgency of the days in which we live. The
New Testament reminds us that ". . . the time is
short . . ." (1 Cor. 7:29), ". . . the days are evil" (Eph.
5:16), ". . . the fields . . . are . . . white . . ." (John 4:35),
". . . the laborers are few" (Matt. 9:37), ". . . the night is
coming . . ." (John 9:4), ". . . the coming of the Lord is at
hand" (James 5:8).

Illustration

In Kensington Gardens, one of London's great parks,
there stands an elevated clock which has four dials: each
showing north, south, east, and west. Underneath each
dial two words are carved in large letters: TIME FLIES. There
is only one answer to this sense of urgency: it is the ra-
pidity of winged feet.

III. The Utility of the Divine Method

"How beautiful upon the mountains are the feet of him
who brings good news . . ." (52:7). God's method in com-

municating the gospel has always been *man*. The writer to the Hebrews puts it perfectly when he says: "God, who at various times and in different ways spoke in time past to *the fathers* by *the prophets*, has in these last days spoken to us by His Son . . ." (Heb. 1:1–2). While his method has been man, the manner of presentation has changed with every age. In other words, feet remain the same, but shoe styles change in every century. Solomon could exclaim, "How beautiful are thy feet with shoes, O prince's daughter! . . ." (Song of Sol. 7:1, KJV). And Paul speaks of our feet being shod ". . . with the preparation of the gospel of peace" (Eph. 6:15). Without doubt, his idea of a shoe was a footman's sandal or a Roman war boot. But if he were alive today what term would he use? All this leads us to say that the utility of the divine method is adaptable to the times, but always amenable to the truth.

A. God's Method Is Always Adaptable to the Times

"How beautiful upon the mountains are the feet of him who brings good news . . ." (52:7). When Isaiah caught the vision of the heralds of deliverance, he saw feet that were simply beautiful. According to Dr. J. A. Alexander, that word "beautiful" can be translated "suitable," "becoming," or "appropriate." Had Isaiah been living in our day he would see winged feet of another style altogether. Instead of the sandals of footmen, or the glittering hoofs of horses, he would see the wings of the modern jet skimming over the mountains for a perfect landing. He would see the towers of powerful radio transmitters carrying the message around the world.

God's message is still the gospel. God's mission is still to reach the world. God's method is still man, but his shoes are up-to-date. We live in an age of technology and amazing scientific advances, and we must thank God for these discoveries. Instead of condemning them, or ignoring them, we *must* employ them to wing the message around the world. This is the only answer to the crisis days in which we live. Without a return to God, on the part of people in every nation under heaven, there is no hope of averting another global conflict. We must use the jet, we must use the powerful transmitters, we must use satellite; in fact, everything and anything to reach the world with the gospel. Our motto should be: "To every creature . . . by every possible means" (see Mark 16:15; 1 Cor. 9:22, PHILLIPS). This is adaptability to the changing times, and we must not allow prejudice, pride, poverty, or pessimism to defeat God's purposes.

Illustration

A high school in Virginia offered a course called "Home Economics for Boys." Needless to say, it got little attention. So the following year it was renamed "Bachelor Living." You guessed it! The effect was overwhelming—120 boys promptly signed up. The curriculum never changed. It still offered traditional instruction in cooking, sewing, laundry, and money management. But it needed the right image before the students would give the class a second look.

As we present Christ to the world, let's not forget that the message must never change, but the methods may vary.[2]

B. God's Method Is Always Amenable to the Truth

"How beautiful upon the mountains are the feet of him who brings good news . . ." (52:7). However we may adjust to the changing times does not alter the changeless truth. Paul reminds us that ". . . we can do nothing against the truth, but for the truth" (2 Cor. 13:8); and again: ". . . if anyone preaches any other gospel to you than what you have received, let him be accursed" (Gal. 1:9). Once more we are reminded to ". . . contend earnestly for the faith . . . once for all delivered to the saints" (Jude 3).

In every age we shall be criticized for being funda-
mentalists or evangelicals, but, undaunted, we must
contend for the truth. God's revelation is unaffected by
the passing years, human speculation, or scientific
advances. It is the one eternal gospel. The shoes of the
herald may change, but the message he brings is ever
the same. It is time the Christian public realized this
and began to support those who truly preach the gospel.
Unfortunately, the average Christian is so gullible that he
nestles comfortably in any church where he takes a
fancy to the minister's personality and easy-going
preaching which makes no demands on anyone.

Conclusion

It is time to awake and put on strength; to shake ourselves from the dust, and make known the only gospel that
can save a lost world (see 52:1–2). We need winged feet
for the universality of the message, the urgency of the mission, and the utility of the method. Are you ready to be
one of those heralds by yielding your life, your talents,
time, and tithes?

Thanksgiving:
Counting Our Blessings
Psalm 103

"Bless the LORD, O my soul, and forget not all his benefits" (103:2).

Introduction

This hymn of praise is without a peer in all the world's literature. It is the language of a man who has stirred up his soul to contemplate the goodness and faithfulness of his God. His words are untouched by sorrow, complaint, or selfishness. From beginning to end, the stanzas cascade like a torrent of thanksgiving. Indeed, the psalm has been compared to a stream that gradually acquires strength and volume till its waves of praise swell like those of the sea. Underlying the magnificence of this poetic movement is the call to count our blessings day by day. The psalmist tells us that with thankful hearts:

I. We Are to Eulogize the Attributes of God

"Bless the LORD, O my soul; and all that is within me, bless His holy name!" (103:1). This is where every soul must start. Before we can thank God for his blessings we must thank him for his being; and this is what the psalmist commands us to do. He urges us to engage all our intellectual, emotional, and volitional powers in blessing and magnifying the holy name of our God. The phrase, "His holy name" (103:1), embraces every attribute of the person and nature of our God. As we survey these essential and moral excellencies and virtues of God, as revealed in his Word—and especially in his Son—we cannot but be "lost in wonder, love, and praise."

Illustration

Dr. A. W. Tozer "was a worshiper—one whose heart was fixed on God continually, who wanted to know him more than he wanted any other thing in life. His work and ministry, his preaching and writing, his personal and public life all revolved around five words: 'I fell down to worship' (Rev. 22:8). . . . Sometimes he would kneel with his face lifted; other times he would lie on the floor, a piece of white paper under his face to prevent breathing carpet dust. He saw the beauty and glory of the Trinity, and in kaleidoscopic splendor he would see this attribute and the other pass before his raptured sight . . ." Is it any wonder that he became such a mighty prophet who earned the right to be heard by the whole church of Christ?[1]

In a day when men and women are encouraged to adopt unworthy views of God and of his Word, it is both important and wholesome that we come to such a psalm as this in order to condition ourselves afresh in the holy art of worship. Jesus declared, "God is Spirit, and those who worship Him must worship in spirit and truth" (John 4:24). May we then be given both the spiritual attitude and the biblical knowledge to eulogize the attributes of our God.

II. We Are to Itemize the Benefits of God

"Bless the LORD, O my soul, and forget not all His benefits" (103:2). One of the evidences of the havoc which sin
has caused in our lives is that we are such creatures of for-
getfulness. Whether in times of failure or of success, we
tend to overlook the constant blessings which God lav-
ishes upon us. So the divine poet exhorts us not to forget
all his benefits. Indeed, we are to itemize both the personal, as well as the national, benefits of our God.

William Law, in his *Serious Call to a Devout and Holy
Life* writes, "Would you know who is the greatest saint in
the world? It is not he who prays most or fasts most; it is
not he who gives most alms, or is most eminent for tem-
perance, chastity, or justice, but it is he who is always
thankful to God, who wills everything that God willeth,
who receives everything as an instance of God's goodness,
and has a heart always ready to praise God for it."

Consider first:

The Personal Blessings

A. There Is the Personal Blessing of Absolution

"Who forgives all your iniquities" (103:3). There is
only one who can absolve sins and that is God, through
his Son Jesus Christ our Lord. The Savior declared:
". . . the Son of Man has power on earth to forgive
sins . . ." (Matt. 9:6).

Have you been forgiven? Do you know the peace of
a pardoned life? Can you say with David: "Blessed is
he whose transgression is forgiven, whose sin is cov-
ered" (Ps. 32:1)? Can you itemize this blessing in your
life? Needless to say, it is basic to all other blessings.
Without forgiveness nothing else can follow.

Illustration

The Duke of Wellington was about to pronounce the death sentence on a confirmed deserter. Deeply moved, the great general said, "I am extremely sorry to pass this severe sentence, but we have tried everything, and all the discipline and penalties have failed to improve this man who is otherwise a brave and good soldier." Then he gave the man's comrades an opportunity to speak for him. "Please, your Excellency," said one of the men, "there is one thing you have never tried. You have not tried forgiving him." The general forgave him and it worked: the soldier never again deserted and ever after showed his gratitude to the Iron Duke.[2]

B. There Is the Personal Blessing of Restoration

". . . Who heals all your diseases" (103:3). Now while the thought of sickness is not entirely absent from this statement the main idea is that of moral defilement; so the psalmist follows the promise of absolution with the word of restoration. John, in his epistle, combines these two blessings when he says, "If we confess our sins, He is faithful and just to forgive us our sins and to cleanse us from all unrighteousness" (1 John 1:9). Forgiveness is absolution; cleansing is restoration. How wonderful to know that the blood of Jesus Christ, God's Son, goes on cleansing and restoring us as we walk in the light of obedience.

C. There Is the Personal Blessing of Elevation

"Who redeems your life from destruction . . ."; or more literally, "Who saves, or rescues, thy life from the pit" (103:4). David has the same thought in mind in Psalm 40:1–2 when he says: "I waited patiently for the Lord; and He inclined to me, and heard my cry. He also brought me up out of a horrible pit, out of the miry clay, and set my feet upon a rock. . . ." Thank God for the elevated place to which he brings his people. Paul describes this as being ". . . made [to] sit together in heavenly places in Christ Jesus" (Eph. 2:6).

D. There Is the Personal Blessing of Coronation

". . . Who crowns you with lovingkindness and tender mercies" (103:4). This is a metaphor drawn from the common custom of wearing wreaths and garlands on festive occasions (see Ps. 8:5). Having elevated us, our God makes us "kings and priests" to himself (see Rev. 1:6). In New Testament language, this is nothing more or less than reigning ". . . in life through the One, Jesus Christ" (Rom. 5:17).

E. There Is the Personal Blessing of Satisfaction

"Who satisfies your mouth with good things, so that your youth is renewed like the eagle's" (103:5). Such is the rejuvenating effect of God's satisfying blessing in Christ that our youth is renewed like the eagle's. The reference here, of course, is to the fresh and vigorous appearance of the eagle when it receives its new plumage. Isaiah reminds us that ". . . those who wait on the LORD shall renew their strength; they shall mount up with wings like eagles . . ." (Isa. 40:31).

These, then, are the *personal* blessings that we are to itemize. Let us see to it that we never forget, or overlook, what God is constantly doing for us through Jesus Christ our Lord.

Illustration

A father and his little girl were walking together one clear, wintry night. The little girl said, "Father, I am going to count the stars." The father heard her count to two hundred and twenty-five. Then he heard her sigh, "O dear, I had no idea there were so many. I don't believe I can ever count them all!" The wise father answered, "The stars are just like God's benefits. God showers us with his blessings and benefits day by day. There are so many of them that we can never count them all."[3]

The National Blessings

A. There Is the National Blessing of God's Justice

"The Lord executes righteousness and justice for all who are oppressed. He made known his ways to Moses, His acts to the children of Israel" when he brought them out of bondage, through the wilderness and into the Promised Land (103:6–7). Such divine intervention has been repeated times without number throughout the history of the human race. God is still the Judge of all the earth, and we can trust him to do righteously when we call upon his name. This is Paul's burden in 1 Timothy 2:1–4: ". . . I exhort first of all that supplications, prayers, intercessions, and giving of thanks be made for all men, for kings and all who are in authority, that we may lead a quiet and peaceable life in all godliness and reverence. For this is good and acceptable in the sight of God our Savior, who desires all men to be saved and to come to the knowledge of the truth."

Illustration

A modern-day intervention of God was recounted by a missionary from Indonesia. It seems that in August, 1965, the President of that country became ill and news of this leaked through to Peking, who saw this as their opportunity to organize a coup. Plans were set in motion and all who stood in the way were liquidated. Lists were drawn up of those who should be killed after the takeover, and this included missionaries who were active in that land. In fact, mass graves had been dug two months before September 30th (the target date) so that bodies could be easily disposed of. Without full knowledge of what was going on in the capital, a humble pastor in an obscure part of the country was burdened to pray. Calling his members together, he asked them to pray and fast with him, and not return to work until God had lifted the burden of prayer from his heart. A day went by, then a second, and then a third. At last he announced, "Victory has come. You may return to your homes and to your jobs." Later he visited one of the missionaries down river and told his story. He confessed he had never known such a burden, nor had he received such an assurance of resounding triumph. Amazed, the missionary checked the dates and learned that the hour of victory coincided with the collapse of the communist coup.

B. There Is the National Blessing of God's Mercy

"The LORD is merciful and gracious, slow to anger, and abounding in mercy" (103:8). Having made this statement concerning God's blessing of mercy, as revealed to Moses (see Exod. 34:6), the psalmist proceeds to demonstrate the outworking of divine mercy:

1. THERE IS THE MERCY OF GOD'S PATIENCE

"He will not always strive with us, nor will He keep his anger forever. He has not dealt with us according to our sins. nor punished us according to our iniquities" (103:9–10). But for the longsuffering and patience of God, every nation under heaven would have been annihilated. God, in wrath, remembers mercy and waits patiently for nations to repent and to seek his face.

2. THERE IS THE MERCY OF GOD'S PARDON

"For as the heavens are high above the earth, so great is His mercy toward those who fear Him; as far as the east is from the west, so far has He removed our transgressions from us" (103:11–12). There is such a thing as national sin, as well as personal sin. The Bible says, "Righteousness exalts a nation, but sin is a reproach to any people" (Prov. 14:34). Thank God that upon true repentance God is willing to forgive a nation as well as an individual. He longs to bless the peoples of the earth.

3. THERE IS THE MERCY OF GOD'S PITY

"As a father pities his children, so the LORD pities those who fear Him" (103:13). The psalmist then goes on to discuss the frailty and brevity of man's human existence (see vv. 14–18). He is compared to the grass that grows up one day and is scorched the next; and yet in mercy and pity God looks down upon man in all his weakness and blesses all who keep his covenant and obeys his commandments.

4. THERE IS THE MERCY OF GOD'S POWER

"The LORD has established His throne in heaven, and His kingdom rules over all" (103:19). Here is an aspect of God's mercy which is ignored by nations today—including so-called Christian countries. If only we believed that God omnipotent reigneth, and that he causes wars to cease in response to the prevailing prayers of his people, we would see the same miracles happen in our day that were witnessed by Moses and the children of Israel. The trouble with us is that we have forgotten our national blessings. We no longer recognize the God of justice and mercy. Thanksgiving has become a hollow and meaningless word. Would to God we returned to the letter and spirit of this mighty psalm!

Illustration

During colonial days the British settlements in New England were under constant attack by the French. One day word came that a mighty armada of 40 ships was setting out from Nova Scotia to conquer the colonies and claim the territory of New England for France. Our pious forefathers called a day of repentance and prayer. In the Old South Church in Boston they laid hold of God. While they were praying, a wind suddenly sprang up. The group pleaded with the Almighty Creator that the wind might be utilized for the destruction of the invading fleet. The wind grew into a mighty storm and then into a hurricane, so powerful that the invading armada, under the command of Duke D'Anville found a watery grave along the rock-bound coast of New England.

III. We Must Recognize the Purposes of God

"Bless the LORD, you His angels, . . . bless the LORD, all you His hosts, . . . Bless the LORD, all His works, . . . Bless the LORD, O my soul!" (103:20–22). The psalmist climaxes his paean of praise by calling upon angels in heaven and men on earth to recognize the purposes of God throughout his universe and throughout time and eternity. No one can appreciate the attributes and benefits of God without desiring above everything else to advance his purposes. We do this by:

A. Obeying God's Word

"Bless the LORD, you His angels, who excel in strength, who do His word!" (103:20). Archangels in heaven, who excel in strength, are engaged unceasingly in obeying the word of their God. We should remember this when we pray that phrase of the Lord's Prayer, ". . . Thy will be done in earth, as it is in heaven" (Matt. 6:10, KJV). A thankful heart always issues in an obedient life. ". . . to obey is better than sacrifice, and to heed than the fat of rams" (1 Sam. 15:22).

Illustration

A Chinese convert declared that he found the best way to remember the Word was to *do* it! . . . he incarnated the Word and it became a vital part of his own personality. He lived it and it lived in him. The Word became flesh. This is the only really vital "way of remembrance," to confirm the Word into the primary stuff of the life.[4]

B. Fulfilling God's Will

"Bless the LORD, all you His hosts, you ministers of His, who do His pleasure" (103:21). If celestial beings that excel in strength are archangels, then the multitude of the host of heaven are angels, whose tireless occupation is that of fulfilling the divine will. Paul tells us that the ultimate expression of total dedication to God is that of proving ". . . what is that good and acceptable and perfect will of God" (Rom. 12:2). That is the only way we please our Lord and live to his glory.

C. Performing God's Work

"Bless the LORD, all His works, in all places of His dominion . . ." (103:22). Here the psalmist has in mind the material universe, including the race of men, and he calls upon every creature of earth to perform his appointed task (see Mark 13:34). Paul reminds us that we are the workmanship of God ". . . created in Christ Jesus for good works, which God prepared beforehand that we should walk in them" (Eph. 2:10).

Illustration

A man dreamed he died and was taken by the angels to a beautiful temple. After admiring it for some time he discovered that one stone was left out and he asked the angel why. The reply was, "That was left out for you; but you wanted to do great things, so there was no room left for you." Startled, he awoke and resolved he would become a worker for God.[5]

True thankfulness of heart issues not only in the obedience of life, but also in the performance of labor, for ". . . we are God's fellow workers . . ." (1 Cor. 3:9).

Conclusion

Counting our blessings is more than mouthing words or even saying prayers. It involves eulogizing the attributes of God, itemizing the benefits of God, and recognizing the purposes of God. If our thankfulness is genuine we shall not only exclaim, "Bless the LORD, O my soul," but we shall go forth to obey God's Word, to fulfill God's will, and to perform his work.

13

Christmas:
The Incarnate Word
John 1:1, 14, 16–18

"The Word became flesh and dwelt among us, and we beheld His glory, the glory as of the only begotten of the Father, full of grace and truth" (1:14).

Introduction

"Life," says Westcott, "is the knowledge of God; and this knowledge lives and moves. It is not a dead thing, embalmed once and for all in phrases." What a description of the Lord Jesus Christ! As "the logos," he truly is the knowledge of God, alive and active. John expresses this concept perfectly in the closing verses of his prologue. His message is that God the Son, who ever was the eternal Word, after having expressed himself as the creative Word by bringing the universe into existence, became the incarnate Word that men and women might have the knowledge of God. What is implied and involved in his

becoming the incarnate Word must now engage our attention. Consider:

I. The Mystery of the Divine Condescension

God's Coming.

"... the Word *became* flesh and dwelt among us ..."
(1:14). To understand the mystery of the divine condescension, we must think of:

A. The Mystery of His Being

"In the beginning was the Word, and the Word was
with God, and the Word was God" (1:1). As the incarnate Word, he was *the Creator of all things*—"All things
were made through Him ..." (1:3). Only God can create,
and without the exercise of his creatorial power nothing
exists apart from himself. In this alone is manifested all
the attributes and characteristics of the eternal power
and Godhead of our Lord Jesus Christ. As we have seen
already, he brought the universe into existence in all
the grandeur of its vastness, as well as the wonder of
its smallness. This is the God who became flesh.

Not only is he the Creator of all things, but also *the
Sustainer of all things*—"... without Him nothing was
made that was made" (1:3). Apart from him nothing can
exist or consist. He upholds "... all things by the word
of His power ..." (Heb. 1:3); "... in Him all things consist" (Col. 1:17).

Illustration

Eugene Cernan, one of the astronauts who enjoyed the
exciting adventure of walking on the moon, said with wonder, "Our world appears big and beautiful, all blue and
white! You can see from the Antarctic to the North Pole.
The earth looks so perfect. *There are no strings to hold it
up; there is no fulcrum upon which it rests.*" Contemplating
the infinity of space and time, he said he felt as if he were

seeing earth from God's perspective when it was created. Yet wonder of wonders, he is the Sustainer of all things; the entire universe is dependent upon him every moment.[1]

The verses before us also show that he is *the Revealer of all things*—"In Him was life, and the life was the light of men. . . . That was the true Light which gives light to every man who comes into the world" (1:4, 9). All knowledge and wisdom have their source in the eternal Son of God (see Col. 2:3, 9). No wonder Paul bursts forth with those glorious words of praise in Romans 11:33–36: "Oh, the depth of the riches both of the wisdom and knowledge of God! How unsearchable are His judgments and His ways past finding out! 'For who has known the mind of the LORD? Or who has become His counselor? Or who has first given to Him and it shall be repaid to him?' For of Him and through Him and to Him are all things, to whom be glory forever. Amen." Yet the amazing fact remains that the Revealer of all things became a learner, for after his birth ". . . Jesus increased in wisdom and stature . . . [learning] obedience by the things which he suffered" (Luke 2:58; Heb. 5:8).

B. The Mystery of His Becoming

". . . the Word became flesh and dwelt among us . . ." (1:14). Man always aspires; God alone condescends. Of God alone can it be said that ". . . He humbled Himself and became obedient to the point of death, even the death of the cross" (Phil. 2:8).

In this becoming he assumed *man's humanity*— ". . . the Word became flesh . . ." (1:14). Carefully observe that the verse does not say he merely became "a man." The Spirit of God is very exact in saying he became flesh; that is, he took upon himself humanity and represented every member of Adam's race. In the language of the apostle Paul, he became the last Adam—"the sec-

ond Man" (1 Cor. 15:47). The body God prepared for
him became not only a garment of deity, but the vehi-
cle of divine expression. Thus he was very God of very
God and very man of very man; the mosaic of humanity
was totalized in him.

> Like man he walked, like God he talked;
> His words were oracles, his deeds were miracles;
> Of God the true expression, of man the finest speci-
>   men;
> Full-orbed humanity, crowned with Deity;
> No trace of infirmity, no taint of iniquity;
> Behold the Man! Behold thy God!
> Veiled in flesh the Godhead see,
> Hail, Incarnate Deity![2]

Furthermore, he assumed *man's adversity*—". . . the
Word became flesh and dwelt among us . . ." (1:14). Only
divine love could condescend to dwell among men; in
fact, his delights were always with the sons of men (see
Rev. 21:3). Such communion started in the Garden of
Eden when God came down to walk and talk with Adam.
Then sin came and severed that holy relationship; but
still God longed to have fellowship with man. Next, we
see him tabernacling with a family under the leadership
of Abraham; later with the nation under the leadership
of Moses (See Exod. 25:8). Finally, John tells us that when
the fullness of time was come, ". . . the Word became
flesh and dwelt [tabernacled] among us . . ." (1:14). What
humility, what condescension, what matchless love!

Jesus was not born in a palace or in a mansion, but
in a simple manger, thus assuming man's adversity. In
his condescension he fulfilled that word: ". . . you know
the grace of our Lord Jesus Christ, that though He was
rich, yet for your sakes He became poor, that you
through His poverty might become rich" (2 Cor. 8:9).
Have you ever noticed that *at birth there was no room
for him* (see Luke 2:7), *in life there was no home for him*

(see Matt. 8:20), and *in death there was no grave for him* (see Matt. 27:59–60)? Truly he shared man's adversity.

> Thou art the Unapproached Whose height
> Enables Thee to stoop,
> Whose holiness is undefiled
> To handle hearts that droop.
> How Thou canst think so well of me
> And be the God Thou art
> Is darkness to my intellect
> But sunshine to my heart.[3]
>
> Frederick W. Faber

But once again, in his condescension, he assumed man's delinquency—". . . the Word became flesh and dwelt among us . . ." (1:14). While he was never a sharer in men's sins, he was a bearer of men's sins. Throughout his life he was ". . . a man of sorrows and acquainted with grief . . ." (Isa. 53:3), and in his death he was made ". . . sin for us, that we might become the righteousness of God in Him" (2 Cor. 5:21). But that is not the whole story. The third day he rose again in order that he might live—or tabernacle—in the hearts of all who will welcome him by faith.

So in the sweep of his condescension we learn that he came to men, he died of men, and he lives in men. What a gracious and glorious condescension! Truly we can exclaim with the apostle Paul: ". . . without controversy great is the mystery of godliness: God was manifested in the flesh, justified in the Spirit, seen by angels, preached among the Gentiles, believed on in the world, received up in glory" (1 Tim. 3:16).

II. The Miracle of the Divine Operation *God's Clothing.*

". . . the Word became flesh . . ." (1:14). The doctrine of the virgin birth is an important one, for the subsequent life and work of Christ stand or fall with the truth of the incarnation. In order to be the Savior of the world the Lord Jesus had to experience:

A. A Sinless Birth

". . . the Word became flesh . . ." (1:14). While born as an infant, the Babe of Bethlehem was not subject to the transmission of original sin (see Matt. 1:20; Luke 1:35). By the overshadowing of the Holy Spirit, that which was begotten in Mary was safeguarded from the contamination of sin. The seed was absolutely holy.

B. A Supernatural Birth

". . . the word became flesh . . ." (1:14). The story of the nativity makes it plain that the mother of Jesus was a virgin, the conception was miraculous, and the agent was the Holy Spirit. In becoming flesh, the Lord Jesus gathered up into himself all the elements of sinless humanity; therefore, no form of human life has an exclusive right to him. This very fact distinguishes Christianity from all other religions since they are all limited to the people among whom they originated; but Christ touches men at every point, through every grade and variety of humanity. In our Lord ". . . there is neither Greek nor Jew, . . . slave nor free, but Christ is all and in all" (Col. 3:11).

Illustration

Italy celebrates Garibaldi, but Italy alone; Germany recalls Bismarck and the old Emperor, but not France; France remembers Napoleon, but England despises him; no foreign nation keeps Washington's birthday. But Jesus belongs unto all the nations of the earth. He reigns supreme as the universal Master.

"This is the biblical interpretation of the person of

Jesus. A naturalistic philosophy necessarily cannot accept this as true. Then that philosophy is called upon to account for Jesus in some other way; and the only way to do that is to do what naturalistic philosophy does: change the Jesus that is presented in this New Testament. To deny the supernatural origin of Jesus is to make him natural merely. To do that invalidates the records, not of his being alone, but of his teaching, and his power in human history. The reason why men reject this story is discovered in their philosophy of God. If he is limited by their knowledge, this thing cannot be. But we are not among the number of those who hold this philosophy of God. We do not think of him as imprisoned within the laws we have discovered, and the forces we know. Therefore the answer of the angel carries our rational consent; because it is the only accounting for him that satisfies our reason" (Dr. G. Campbell Morgan).

III. The Marvel of ~~the Divine Revelation~~ God's Closeness.

". . . the Word became flesh and dwelt among us, and we beheld His glory, the glory as of the only begotten of the Father, full of grace and truth" (1:14). An old Indian once said to Sir John Franklin, the explorer, "I am an old man now, and I have never seen God." Moses could not see the face of God and live, so God had to shelter him with his hand, lest he perish. Elijah was not allowed to see God, so he only heard a still, small voice after the wind, earthquake, and fire. Even John the seer could not look upon God and see him in the visions he was given on the isle of Patmos. The fact is, no man has seen God, or can see God, for he dwells ". . . in unapproachable light . . ." (1 Tim. 6:16). Yet, wonder of wonders, through the coming of Christ into human flesh, we are now able to see God, to know him, and to love him (see 1:18). In this marvel of divine revelation we have:

God's

A. The Beauty of ~~the Divine~~ Expression

". . . the glory as of the only begotten of the Father, full of grace and truth" (1:14). Artists tell us that beauty is made up of curved lines (symbols of the feminine), and the straight lines (symbols of the masculine). The curved represents the concept of grace, while the straight denotes the idea of truth. Thus grace and truth wonderfully combine in one glorious personality of the Lord Jesus Christ.

We see divine grace as he touched the heads of children, or looked into the face of the crushed and broken woman of the street, and said, ". . . Neither do I condemn you; go and sin no more" (John 8:11). But we also see the straight lines of justice, righteousness, and truth, as he challenges the accusers of the same woman with the words, ". . . He who is without sin among you, let him throw a stone at her first." And we read, "Then those who heard it, being convicted by their conscience, went out one by one, beginning with the oldest, even to the last . . ." (John 8:7, 9). In all his ways, grace and truth flashed out from his person, his words, and his works. This was the glory and marvel of the divine revelation.

Illustration

An Alaskan girl was found by her teacher admiring a beautiful sunset. When it was suggested that she try to put the scene on canvas, she replied: "O, I can't draw glory." In the same way, the most expressive words are utterly inadequate to describe the glory and majesty of the incarnate Word, full of grace and truth.

God's

B. The Blessing of ~~the Divine~~ Intention

". . . of His fullness we have all received, and grace for grace" (1:16). Without doubt, verse 16 is linked with verse 12, where John has told us that ". . . as many as received Him, to them He gave the right to become children of God, even to those who believe in His name."

We cannot receive the fullness of God's grace and truth apart from the Lord Jesus (see Col. 2:9–10).

The fullness of grace that resides in him is made available to us and in us by the miracle of his indwelling. This is God's saving grace—"For by grace you have been saved through faith, and that not of yourselves; it is the gift of God" (Eph. 2:8). It is sanctifying grace, for Paul reminds us that by the grace of God we are what we are (see 1 Cor. 15:10). But it is also serving grace, for it is according to the grace of God which is given unto us so that we can be wise master builders (see 1 Cor. 3:10) and servants of the Lord. All this and more is ours because Jesus has come in the flesh to live, to die, to rise again, and then to indwell all who welcome him by simple faith. The wonder of such an indwelling would be almost overwhelming were it not for the fact that the Holy Spirit strengthens our inner man to stand the grandeur and power of this inward revelation (see Eph. 3:14–19). The mere contemplation of this truth should cause us to prostrate ourselves before our God in wonder, love, and praise.

Conclusion

We have seen that the ultimate purpose of God in the incarnation is not only to show us what he is like, but to transform us into that same likeness from glory to glory until at last we reach perfect conformity to the very image of the Son of God himself. Jesus came to where we are in order that we might rise to where he is. His first advent brought about the transformation; the second advent will bring about the consummation (see 1 John 3:1–2).

As we contemplate this mystery of the divine condescension, this miracle of the divine operation, and this marvel of the divine revelation, we are constrained to say, in the words of an ancient prayer: "To Thee, O Christ, O Word of the Father, we offer our lowly praises and unfeigned hearty thanks: Who for love of our fallen race didst most wonderfully and humbly choose to be made man, as never to be *unmade* [again], and to take our nature, as *never more to lay it off*; so that we might be born again by thy Spirit and restored in the image of God; to whom, one blessed Trinity, be ascribed all honor, majesty, and dominion, now and for ever. Amen."

Endnotes

Chapter 2

1. *Pulpit Helps* (Chattanooga, Tenn.: AMG International, Jan. 1981).

2. *House and Garden,* quoted in Paul Lee Tan, *Encyclopedia of 7,700 Illustrations* (Garland, Tex.: Bible Communications, Inc., 1979).

3. M. R. DeHaan, *Our Daily Bread* (Grand Rapids: Radio Bible Class, n.d.).

4. Ibid.

5. *Life of Faith,* in Aquilla Webb, *1,000 New Illustrations* (New York: Harper and Row).

6. Amy Wilson Carmichael, Christian Literature Crusade, Fort Washington, Pennsylvania.

Chapter 3

1. Paul Lee Tan, *Encyclopedia of 7,700 Illustrations* (Garland, Tex.: Bible Communications, Inc., 1979), p. 1227.

2. Ibid., 663.

3. James C. Hefley, *Prophetic Witness*, vol. 8, no. 3 (Loughborough, England: Prophetic Witness Publishing House, March 1984), p. 15.

4. Tan, *Encyclopedia of 7,700 Illustrations,* p. 1190.

Chapter 4

1. *Sermons Illustrated* (Holland, Ohio, Feb. 11, 1987).

2. Ibid., July 18, 1986.

3. *King's Business,* quoted in Paul Lee Tan, *Encyclopedia of 7,700 Illustrations* (Garland, Tex.: Bible Communications, Inc., 1979), p. 1177.

4. Russel Sewall, ibid., 1157.

5. Robert A. Cole, *The Gospel According to St. Mark* (Tyndale New Testament Commentaries), p. 238.

6. Ibid.

Chapter 5

1. *Day by Day with Jesus* (St. Louis: Concordia, 1980).
2. W. E. Sangster, *The Craft of Sermon Illustration* (London: Epworth, 1946), p. 19.
3. David C. Egner, *Our Daily Bread* (Grand Rapids: Radio Bible Class, Nov. 18, 1982).

Chapter 6

1. *Day by Day with Jesus* (St. Louis: Concordia, 1981).
2. J. Sidlow Baxter, *The Master Theme of the Bible* (Wheaton, Ill.: Tyndale).
3. *Day by Day with Jesus* (St. Louis: Concordia, 1979).
4. Ibid.

Chapter 7

1. *Day by Day with Jesus* (St. Louis: Concordia, 1979).

Chapter 9

1. Dennis J. DeHaan, *Our Daily Bread* (Grand Rapids: Radio Bible Class, May 13, 1979).

Chapter 10

1. A. Naismith, *1,200 Notes, Quotes, and Anecdotes* (Hammersmith: Pickering & Inglis, 1963), p. 179.
2. Dan Yeary, "Does Your Job Mean More Than Pay?" *Harvest Today* (Coral Gables, Fla.: World Team, Fall/Winter 1981), p. 4.
3. *The Sermon Builder*, quoted in *Pulpit Helps* (Chattanooga, Tenn: AMG International, Dec. 1985), adapted.
4. *Choice Gleanings* (Grand Rapids: Gospel Folio Press, Feb. 3, 1983).
5. Naismith, *1200 Notes, Quotes, and Anecdotes,* p. 193.
6. Copyright Salvationist Publishing and Supplies, Ltd., London, England.

Chapter 11

1. Walter B. Knight, *Knight's Master Book of New Illustrations* (Grand Rapids: Eerdmans, 1956), p. 256.
2. *Sermons Illustrated* (Spearman, Tex., April 7, 1986).

Chapter 12

1. Raymond McAfee, "He Fell Down to Worship," *The Alliance Witness* (July 24, 1963), pp 8–9.

2. A. Naismith, *1,200 Notes, Quotes, and Anecdotes* (Hammersmith: Pickering & Inglis, 1963), p. 72.

3. Adapted from the *Pentecostal Evangel* (Springfield, Mo., n.d.).

4. John Henry Jowett, *My Daily Meditation,* p. 132.

5. Dwight L. Moody, quoted in Paul Lee Tan, *Encyclopedia of 7,700 Illustrations* (Garland, Tex: Bible Communications, Inc., 1979), p. 1630, adapted.

Chapter 13

1. *Sermons Illustrated* (Spearman, Tex., Mar. 23, 1986).

2. A. Naismith, *1,200 Notes, Quotes, and Anecdotes* (Hammersmith: Pickering & Inglis, 1963), p. 40.

3. Ibid.

For Further Reading

Chapter 1

Alexander, J. A. *Commentary on the Prophecies of Isaiah.* Grand Rapids: Zondervan Publishing House, 1962.

Allis, O. T. *The Unity of Isaiah.* Philadelphia: Presbyterian and Reformed Publishing Co., 1950.

Delitzsch, Franz. *Commentary on Isaiah.* 2 vols. Reprint ed. Grand Rapids: Wm. B. Eerdmans Publishing Co., 1949.

Ironside, H. A. *Expository Notes on the Prophet Isaiah.* Neptune, N.J.: Loizeaux Brothers, Inc., 1966.

Jennings, F. C. *Studies in Isaiah.* Neptune, N.J.: Loizeaux Brothers, Inc., 1966.

Vine, W. E. *Isaiah: Prophecies, Promises, Warning.* London: Oliphants, Ltd., 1953.

Young, Edward J. *Studies in Isaiah.* Grand Rapids: Wm. B. Eerdmans Publishing Co., 1954.

Chapter 2

Barclay, William. *Daily Study Bible* (Philippians, Colossians, and Thessalonians). Rev. ed. Philadelphia: Westminster Press, 1975–1976.

Ironside, H. A. *Notes on Philippians.* Neptune, N.J.: Loizeaux Brothers, Inc.

Klug, Ron. *Philippians: God's Guide to Joy.* Fisherman Bible Studyguide Series. Wheaton, Ill.: Harold Shaw Publishers, 1981.

Martin, Ralph. *The Epistle of Paul to the Philippians.* Grand Rapids: Wm. B. Eerdmans Publishing Co., 1978.

Meyer, F. B. *The Epistle to the Philippians.* Grand Rapids: Zondervan Publishing House, 1952.

Vaughan, Charles J. *Epistle to the Philippians.* Minneapolis: Klock and Klock Christian Publishers, 1984.

Wuest, Kenneth S. *Philippians in the Greek New Testament.* Grand Rapids: Wm. B. Eerdmans Publishing Co., 1953.

Chapter 3

Cochrane, Elvis E. *The Epistles of Peter.* Grand Rapids: Baker Book House, 1965.

Cramer, George H. *First and Second Peter.* Chicago: Moody Press, 1967.

Exell, Joseph S., ed. *The Biblical Illustrator on 1 Peter.* Grand Rapids: Baker Book House, 1963.

Jowett, John Henry. *The Epistles of St. Peter. The Practical Commentary on the New Testament.* 1906. Reprint. Grand Rapids: Kregel Publications, 1970.

Rees, Paul S. *Triumphant in Trouble.* Old Tappan, N.J.: Fleming H. Revell, 1962.

Spence, H. D. M. and Joseph S. Exell, eds. *The Pulpit Commentary on 1 Peter.* Grand Rapids: Wm. B. Eerdmans Publishing Co.

Stibbs, Alan. *First Epistle of Peter.* Tyndale New Testament Commentaries. Grand Rapids: Wm. B. Eerdmans Publishing Co., 1960.

Thomas, W. Griffith. *The Apostle Peter: Outline Studies.* Grand Rapids: Wm. B. Eerdmans Publishing Co., 1956.

Chapter 4

Barclay, William. *Daily Study Bible* (Matthew). Rev. ed. Philadelphia: Westminster Press, 1975–1976.

Morgan, G. Campbell. *The Gospel According to Matthew.* New York: Fleming H. Revell, 1929.

Spurgeon, C. H. *The Gospel of the Kingdom.* Grand Rapids: Zondervan Publishing House, reprint, 1962.

Tasker, R. V. G. *The Gospel According to St. Matthew.* Tyndale New Testament Commentaries. Grand Rapids: Wm. B. Eerdmans Publishing Co., 1961.

Walvoord, J. F. *Matthew: Thy Kingdom Come.* Chicago: Moody Press, 1974.

Chapter 5

Alexander, J. A. *Commentary on the Gospel of Mark (CCL).* 1864. Reprint. Grand Rapids: Zondervan Publishing House.

Cole, Robert A. *The Gospel According to St. Mark.* Tyndale New Testament Commentaries. Grand Rapids: Wm. B. Eerdmans Publishing Co., 1961.

English, E. Schuyler. *Studies in the Gospel According to Mark: A Comprehensive Exposition of the Gospel of the Servant-Son of God.* New York: Our Hope, 1943.

Ironside, H. A. *Addresses on the Gospel of Mark.* Neptune, N.J.: Loizeaux Brothers, Inc.

Ryle, John Charles. *Expository Thoughts on the Gospel of Mark.* Carlisle, Pa.: Banner of Truth Trust, 1985.

Swete, Henry Barclay. *Commentary on Mark.* Grand Rapids: Kregel Publications, 1977.

Taylor, Vincent. *The Gospel According to St. Mark.* London: Macmillan Co., 1963.

Chapter 6

Alexander, J. A. *Commentary on the Prophecies of Isaiah.* Grand Rapids: Zondervan Publishing House, 1962.

Allis, O. T. *The Unity of Isaiah.* Philadelphia: Presbyterian and Reformed Publishing Co., 1950.

Criswell, W. A. *Isaiah: An Exposition.* Grand Rapids: Zondervan Publishing House, 1977.

Delitzsch. Franz. *Commentary on Isaiah.* 2 vols. Reprint. Grand Rapids: Wm. B. Eerdmans Publishing Co., 1949.

Ironside, H. A. *Expository Notes on the Prophet Isaiah.* Neptune, N.J.: Loizeaux Brothers, Inc., 1966.

Jennings, F. C. *Studies in Isaiah.* Neptune, N.J.: Loizeaux Brothers, Inc., 1966.

Meyer, F. B. *Christ in Isaiah.* 1895. Reprint. Fort Washington, Pa.: Christian Literature Crusade, 1970.

Redpath, Alan. *Faith for the Times.* 3 vols. Old Tappan, N.J.: Fleming H. Revell Co., 1972, 1974, 1976.

Wiersbe, W. W. *His Name is Wonderful.* Wheaton, IL: Tyndale House Publishers, Inc., 1976.

Young, Edward J. *The Book of Isaiah.* New International Commentary on the Old Testament. 3 vols. Grand Rapids: Wm. B. Eerdmans Publishing Co., 1965–1972.

Chapter 7

Barclay, William. *Daily Study Bible* (John). Rev. ed. Philadelphia: Westminster Press, 1975–1976.

Hendrikson, William. *A Commentary on the Gospel of John.* New Testament Commentary. 2 vols. Grand Rapids: Baker Book House, 1953.

Ironside, H. A. *Addresses on the Gospel of John.* Neptune, N.J.: Loizeaux Brothers, Inc.

Macaulay, J. C. *Expository Commentary on John.* Chicago: Moody Press, 1978.

Morgan, G. Campbell. *The Gospel According to John.* Westwood, N.J.: Fleming H. Revell Co., 1933.

Pink, Arthur W. *Exposition of the Gospel of John.* 4 vols. 1923ff. Reprint. 1 vol. Grand Rapids: Zondervan Publishing House, 1975.

Tasker, R. V. G. *The Gospel According to St. John, an Introduction and Commentary.* Tyndale New Testament Commentaries. Grand Rapids: Wm. B. Eerdmans Publishing Co., 1960.

Tenney, Merrill C. *John: The Gospel of Belief.* Grand Rapids: Wm. B. Eerdmans Publishing Co., 1948.

Westcott, B. F. *The Gospel According to John.* Grand Rapids: Wm. B. Eerdmans Publishing Co., 1962.

Chapters 8 and 9

Barclay, William. *Daily Study Bible* (The Letters to Timothy, Titus, and Philemon). Rev. ed. Philadelphia: Westminster Press, 1975–1976.

Easton, Burton Scott. *The Pastoral Epistles.* London: SCM Press, 1948.

Fairbairn, Patrick. *Commentary on the Pastoral Epistles.* Grand Rapids: Zondervan Publishing House, 1956.

Guthrie, Donald. *The Pastoral Epistles.* Tyndale New Testament Commentaries. Grand Rapids: Wm. B. Eerdmans Publishing Co., 1957.

Hendriksen, William. *Exposition of the Pastoral Epistles.* New Testament Commentary. Grand Rapids: Baker Book House, 1968.

Hiebert, D. Edmond. *Second Timothy.* Chicago: Moody Press, 1958.

Chapter 10

Barclay, William. *Daily Study Bible* (John). Rev. ed. Philadelphia: Westminster Press, 1975–1976.

Hendricksen, William. *A Commentary on the Gospel of John.* New Testament Commentary, 2 vols. Grand Rapids, Baker Book House, 1953.

Ironside, H. A. *Addresses on the Gospel of John.* Neptune, N.J.: Loizeaux Brothers, Inc.

Macaulay, J. C. *Expository Commentary on John.* Chicago: Moody Press, 1978.

Morgan, G. Campbell. *The Gospel According to John.* Westwood, N.J.: Fleming H. Revell Co., 1933.

Pink, Arthur W. *Exposition of the Gospel of John.* 4 vols. 1923ff. Reprint. 1 vol. Grand Rapids: Zondervan Publishing House, 1975.

Tasker, R. V. G. *The Gospel According to St. John, an Introduction and Commentary.* Tyndale New Testament Commentaries. Grand Rapids: Wm. B. Eerdmans Publishing Co., 1960.

Tenney, Merrill C. *John: The Gospel of Belief.* Grand Rapids: Wm. B. Eerdmans Publishing Co., 1948.

Westcott, B. F. *The Gospel According to John.* Grand Rapids: Wm. B. Eerdmans Publishing Co., 1962.

Chapter 11

Alexander, J. A. *Commentary on the Prophecies of Isaiah.* Grand Rapids: Zondervan Publishing House, 1962.

Allis, O. T. *The Unity of Isaiah.* Philadelphia: Presbyterian and Reformed Publishing Co., 1950.

Delitzsch, Franz. *Commentary on Isaiah.* 2 vols. Reprint. Grand Rapids: Wm. B. Eerdmans Publishing Co., 1949.

Ironside, H. A. *Expository Notes on the Prophet Isaiah.* Neptune, N.J.: Loizeaux Brothers, Inc.

Young, Edward J. *The Book of Isaiah.* New International Commentary on the Old Testament. 3 vols. Grand Rapids: Wm. B. Eerdmans Publishing Co., 1965–1972.

Chapter 12

Alexander, Joseph Addison. *The Psalms Translated and Explained.* Reprint from the edition of 1864. Grand Rapids: Zondervan Publishing House.

Delitzsch, Franz. *Biblical Commentary on the Psalms.* Trans. by Francis Bolton. 3 vols. Grand Rapids: Wm. B. Eerdmans Publishing Co., 1949.

Dickson, David. *A Commentary on the Psalms.* 2 vols. Minneapolis: Klock and Klock Christian Publishers, 1980.

Ironside, H. A. *Studies on Psalms: Book One.* Neptune, N.J.: Loizeaux Brothers, Inc., 1952.

Kidner, Derek. *Psalms: An Introduction and Commentary on Books I and II.* Tyndale Old Testament Commentaries. Downers Grove, Ill.: InterVarsity Press, 1973.

Klug, Ron. *Psalms: A Guide to Prayer and Praise.* Fisherman Bible Studyguide Series. Wheaton, Ill.: Harold Shaw Publishers, 1979.

Maclaren, Alexander. *The Psalms.* 3 vols. Minneapolis: Klock and Klock Christian Publishers, 1980.

Morgan, G. Campbell. *Notes on the Psalms.* New York: Fleming H. Revell Co., 1947.

Patterson, John. *The Praises of Israel.* Totowa, N.J.: Charles Scribner's Sons, 1950.

Scroggie, W. Graham. *Know Your Bible* (The Psalms). Vols. 1–4, New York: Fleming H. Revell Co., 1948.

Spurgeon, Charles. *The Treasury of David.* 6 vols. Grand Rapids: Zondervan Publishing House, 1963.

Terrien, Samuel. *The Psalms and Their Meaning for Today.* New York: The Bobbs-Merrill Co., 1952.

Walker, H. Rollin. *The Modern Message of the Psalms.* Nashville: Abingdon Press, 1938.

Weiser, Arthur. *The Psalms: A Commentary.* Trans. from the German. London: SCM Press, 1962.

Chapter 13

Barclay, William. *Daily Study Bible* (John). Rev. ed. Philadelphia: Westminster Press, 1975–1976.

Hendriksen, William. *A Commentary on the Gospel of John.* New Testament Commentary. 2 vols. Grand Rapids: Baker Book House, 1953.

Ironside, H. A. *Addresses on the Gospel of John.* Neptune, N.J.: Loizeaux Brothers, Inc.

Macaulay, J. C. *Expository Commentary on John.* Chicago: Moody Press, 1978.

Morgan, G. Campbell. *The Gospel According to John.* Westwood, N.J.: Fleming H. Revell Co., 1933.

Pink, Arthur W. *Exposition of the Gospel of John.* 4 vols. 1923ff. Reprint. 1 vol. Grand Rapids: Zondervan Publishing House, 1975.

Tasker, R. V. G. *The Gospel According to St. John, an Introduction and Commentary.* Tyndale New Testament Commentaries. Grand Rapids: Wm. B. Eerdmans Publishing Co., 1960.

Tenney, Merrill C. *John: The Gospel of Belief.* Grand Rapids: Wm. B. Eerdmans Publishing Co., 1948.

Westcott, B. F. *The Gospel According to John.* Grand Rapids: Wm. B. Eerdmans Publishing Co., 1962.